Anonymous

A Pair of Blue Eyes

Vol. II

Anonymous

A Pair of Blue Eyes
Vol. II

ISBN/EAN: 9783337040543

Printed in Europe, USA, Canada, Australia, Japan

Cover: Foto ©ninafisch / pixelio.de

More available books at **www.hansebooks.com**

A PAIR OF BLUE EYES.

A Novel.

By THOMAS HARDY,
AUTHOR OF
'UNDER THE GREENWOOD TREE,' 'DESPERATE REMEDIES,' ETC.

'A violet in the youth of primy nature,
Forward, not permanent, sweet, not lasting,
The perfume and suppliance of a minute;
No more.'

IN THREE VOLUMES.

VOL. II.

LONDON:
TINSLEY BROTHERS, 8 CATHERINE ST. STRAND.
1873.

[The right of translation and reproduction is reserved.]

CONTENTS OF VOL. II.

CHAP.		PAGE
I.	'We frolic while 'tis May'	1
II.	'A wandering Voice'	24
III.	'Then Fancy shapes—as Fancy can'	32
IV.	'Her Welcome, spoke in faltering Phrase'	44
V.	'He heard her musical Pants'	62
VI.	'Love was in the next Degree'	101
VII.	'A distant Dearness in the Hill'	123
VIII.	'On thy cold gray Stones, O Sea!'	159
IX.	'Love will find out the Way'	180
X.	'Should auld Acquaintance be forgot?'	204
XI.	'Breeze, Bird, and Flower confess the Hour'	233
XII.	'Mine own familiar Friend'	241
XIII.	'To that last Nothing under Earth'	261
XIV.	'How should I greet thee?'	276

A PAIR OF BLUE EYES.

CHAPTER I.

'WE FROLIC WHILE 'TIS MAY.'

It has now to be not only supposed but clearly realised that nearly three-quarters of a year have passed away. In place of the autumnal scenery which formed a setting to the previous enactments, we have the culminating blooms of summer in the year following.

Stephen is in India, slaving away at an office in Bombay; occasionally going up the country on professional errands, and wondering why people complained so much of the effect of the climate upon their constitutions. Never had a young man a finer start than seemed now to present itself to Stephen. It was just in that exceptional heyday of prosperity which shone over Bombay about ten years ago, that he arrived on the scene. Building and engineering partook of the general impetus. Speculation moved with an accelerated velocity every successive day, the only disagreeable contingency connected with it being the possibility of a capsize.

Elfride had never told her father of the four-and-twenty-hours' escapade with Stephen, nor had it, to her knowledge, come to his ears by any other route. It was a secret trouble and grief to the girl for a short time, and Stephen's departure was another ingredient in her sorrow. But Elfride possessed special facilities for getting rid of trouble after a decent interval. Whilst a slow nature was imbibing a misfortune little by little, she had swallowed the whole agony of it at a draught and was brightening again. She could slough off a sadness and replace it by a hope as easily as a lizard renews a diseased limb.

And two such excellent distractions had presented themselves. One was bringing out the romance and looking for notices in the papers, which, though they had been significantly short so far, had served to divert her thoughts. The other was migrating from the vicarage to the more commodious old house of Mrs. Swancourt's overlooking the same valley. Mr. Swancourt at first disliked the idea of transplantation to feminine soil, but the obvious advantages of such an accession of dignity reconciled him to the change. So there was a radical 'move;' the two ladies staying at Torquay as had been arranged, the vicar going to and fro.

Mrs. Swancourt considerably enlarged Elfride's ideas in an aristocratic direction, and she began to forgive her father for his politic marriage. Certainly, in a worldly sense, a handsome face at three-and-forty had never served a man in better stead.

The new house at Kensington was ready, and they were all in town.

The Hyde-Park shrubs had been transplanted as usual, the chairs ranked in line, the grass edgings trimmed, the roads made to look as if they were suffering from a heavy thunderstorm; carriages had been called for for the easeful, horses for the brisk, and the Drive and Row were again the groove of gaiety for an hour. We gaze upon the spectacle, at six o'clock on this midsummer afternoon, in a melon-frame atmosphere and beneath a violet sky. The Swancourt equipage formed one in the stream.

Mrs. Swancourt was a talker of talk of the incisive kind, which her low musical voice—the only beautiful point in the old woman—prevented from being wearisome.

'Now,' she said to Elfride, who, like Æneas at Carthage, was full of admiration for the brilliant scene, 'you will find that our companionless state will give us, as it does everybody, an extraordinary power in reading the features of our fellow creatures here. I always am a listener in such places as these—not to the narratives told by my neighbours' tongues, but by their faces—the advantage of which is, that whether I am in Row, Boulevard, Rialto, or Prado, they all speak the same language. I may have acquired some skill in this practice through having been an ugly lonely woman for so many years, with nobody to give me information; a thing you will not consider strange when the parallel case is borne in mind,—how truly people who have no clocks will tell the time of day.'

'Ay, that they will,' said Mr. Swancourt corroboratively. 'I have known labouring men at Endelstow and other farms who had framed complete systems of observation for that purpose. By means of shadows, winds, clouds, the movements of sheep and oxen, the singing of birds, the crowing of cocks, and a hundred other sights and sounds which people with watches in their pockets never know the existence of, they are able to pronounce within ten minutes of the hour almost at any required instant. That reminds me of an old story which I'm afraid is too bad—too bad to repeat.' Here the vicar shook his head and laughed inwardly.

'Tell it—do!' said the ladies.

'I mustn't quite tell it.'

'That's absurd,' said Mrs. Swancourt.

'It was only about a man who, by the same careful system of observation, was known to deceive persons for more than two years into the belief that he kept a barometer by stealth, so exactly did he foretell all changes in the weather by the braying of his ass and the temper of his wife.'

Elfride laughed.

'Exactly,' said Mrs. Swancourt. 'And in just the way that those learnt the signs of nature, I have learnt the language of her illegitimate sister — artificiality; and the fibbing of eyes, the contempt of nose tips, the indignation of back hair, the laughter of clothes, the cynicism of footsteps, and the various emotions lying in walking-stick twirls, hat-liftings, the elevation of parasols, the carriage of umbrellas, become as A B C to me.

'Just look at that daughter's-eldest-sister class of mamma in the carriage across there,' she continued to Elfride, pointing with merely a turn of her eye. 'The absorbing self-consciousness of her position that is shown by her countenance is most humiliating to a lover of one's country. You would hardly believe, would you, that members of a Fashionable World, whose professed zero is far above the highest degree of the humble, could be so ignorant of the elementary instincts of reticence.'

'How?'

'Why, to bear on their faces, as plainly

as on a phylactery, the inscription, "Do, pray, look at the coronet on my panels;" or, "Look at the leaves and pearls in my coronet;" or, "Look at the leaves pure and unmixed in mine. I don't say," they seem to go on saying to the shabby people, "that I wish you to think us connected with the Norman Conquest of you, wretched Nobody-knows-who," or whatever the word of the season is for the poorer inhabitants of the country, "but we are, and there is our crest and significant motto."'

'O Mrs. Swancourt!' said Elfride.

'But I much prefer the manners of my acquaintance of that class to the way some of us, with no title but much wealth, look at the strugglers for gentility. There's a specimen—there's another. The glance in them is modified to "O, moneyless ones, this bracelet I wear, weighing three-quarters of a pound, is real gold! Solid, you know—s, o, l, i, d,—right through to the middle and out at the other side."'

'Really, Charlotte,' said the vicar, 'you see as much in faces as Mr. Puff saw in Lord Burleigh's nod.'

Elfride could not but admire the beauty of her fellow countrywomen, especially since herself and her own few acquaintances had always been slightly sunburnt or marked on the back of the hands by a bramble-scratch at this time of the year.

'And what lovely flowers and leaves they wear in their bonnets!' she exclaimed.

'O, yes,' returned Mrs. Swancourt. 'Some of them are even more striking in colour than any real ones. Look at that beautiful rose worn by the lady inside the rails. Elegant vine-tendrils introduced upon the stem as an improvement upon prickles, and all growing so naturally just over her ear—I say *growing* advisedly, for the pink of the petals and the pink of her handsome cheeks are equally from Nature's hand to the eyes of the most casual observer.'

'But praise them a little, they do deserve it!' said generous Elfride.

'Well, I do. See how the Duchess of —— waves to and fro in her seat, utilising the sway of her barouche by looking forward only when her head is swung forward, with a passive pride which forbids a resistance to the force of circumstance. Look at the pretty pout on the mouths of that family there, retaining no traces of being arranged beforehand, so well is it done. Look at the demure close of the little fists holding the parasols; the tiny alert thumb, sticking up erect against the ivory stem as knowing as can be, the satin of the parasol invariably matching the complexion of the face beneath it, yet seemingly by an accident, which makes the thing so attractive. There's the red book lying on the opposite seat, bespeaking the vast numbers of their acquaintance. And I particularly admire the aspect of that abundantly-daughtered woman on the other side—I mean her look of unconsciousness that the girls are stared at by the walkers, and above all the look of the girls themselves—losing their gaze in the depths of handsome men's eyes without appearing to notice whether they are observing masculine eyes or the leaves of the trees. There's praise for you. But I am only jesting, child—you know that.'

'Piph-ph-ph—how warm it is to be sure!' said Mr. Swancourt, as if his mind were a long distance from all he saw. 'I declare that my watch is so hot that I can scarcely bear to touch it to see what the time is, and all the world smells like the inside of a hat.'

'How the men stare at you, Elfride!' said the elder lady. 'You will kill me quite, I am afraid.'

'Kill you?'

'As a diamond kills an opal in the same setting.'

'I have noticed several ladies and gentlemen looking at me,' said Elfride, artlessly showing her pleasure at being observed.

'My dear, you mustn't say "gentlemen" nowadays,' her stepmother answered in the tones of great concern that so well became her. 'We have handed over "gentlemen" to the lower middle class, where the word is still to be heard at tradesmen's balls and provincial tea-parties, I believe. It is done with here.'

'What must I say, then?'

'"Ladies and *men*" always.'

At this moment appeared in the stream of vehicles moving in the contrary direction a chariot presenting in its general surface the rich indigo hue of a midnight sky, the wheels and margins being picked out in delicate lines of ultramarine; the servants' liveries were dark-blue coats and silver lace, and breeches of neutral Indian red. The whole concern formed an organic whole, and moved along behind a pair of ark-chestnut geldings, who advanced in an indifferently zealous trot, very daintily performed, and occasionally shrugged divers points of their veiny surface as if they were rather above the business.

In this sat a gentleman with no decided characteristics more than that he somewhat resembled a good-natured commercial traveller of the superior class. Beside him was a lady with skim-milky eyes and complexion, belonging to the interesting class of women, where that class merges in the sickly, her greatest pleasure being apparently to enjoy nothing. Opposite this pair sat two little girls in white hats and blue feathers.

The lady saw Elfride, smiled and bowed, and touched her husband's elbow, who turned and received Elfride's movement of recognition with a gallant elevation of his hat. Then the two children held up their arms to Elfride, and laughed gleefully.

'Who is that?'

'Why, Lord Luxellian, isn't it?' said Mrs. Swancourt, who, with the vicar, had been seated with her back towards them.

'Yes,' replied Elfride. 'He is the one man of those I have seen here whom I consider handsomer than papa.'

'Thank you, dear,' said Mr. Swancourt.

'Yes; but your father is so much older. When Lord Luxellian gets a little farther on in life, he won't be half so good-looking as our man.'

'Thank you, dear, likewise,' said Mr. Swancourt.

'See,' exclaimed Elfride, still looking towards them, 'how those little dears want me! Actually one of them is crying for me to come.'

'We were talking of bracelets just now. Look at Lady Luxellian's,' said Mrs. Swancourt, as the Baroness lifted up her arm to support one of the children. 'It is slipping up her arm—too large by half. I hate to see daylight between a bracelet and a wrist; I wonder women haven't better taste.'

'It is not on that account, indeed,' Elfride expostulated. 'It is that her arm has got thin, poor thing. You cannot think how much she has altered in this last twelvemonth.'

The carriages were now nearer together, and there was an exchange of more familiar greetings between the two families. Then the Luxellians crossed over and drew up under the plane-tree, just in the rear of the Swancourts. Lord Luxellian alighted, and came forward with a musical laugh.

It was his attraction, as a man. People liked him for those tones, and forgot that he had no talents. Acquaintances remembered Mr. Swancourt by his manner; they remembered Stephen Smith by his face, Lord Luxellian by his laugh.

Mr. Swancourt made some friendly remarks—among other things upon the heat.

'Yes,' said Lord Luxellian, 'we were

driving by a furrier's window this afternoon, and the sight filled us all with such a sense of suffocation that we were glad to get away. Ha-ha!' He turned to Elfride. 'Miss Swancourt, I have hardly seen or spoken to you since your literary feat was made public. I had no idea a child was taking notes down at quiet Endelstow, or I should certainly have put myself and friends upon our best behaviour. Swancourt, why didn't you give me a hint!'

Elfride fluttered, blushed, laughed, said it was nothing to speak of, &c. &c.

'Well, I think you were rather unfairly treated by the *Present;* I certainly do. Writing a heavy review like that upon an elegant trifle like the *Court of Kellyon Castle* was absurd.'

'What?' said Elfride, opening her eyes. 'Was I reviewed in the *Present?*'

'O, yes; didn't you see it? Why, it was four or five months ago!'

'No, I never saw it. How sorry I am!

What a shame of my publishers! They promised to send me every notice that appeared.'

'Ah, then I am almost afraid I have been giving you disagreeable information, intentionally withheld out of courtesy. Depend upon it they thought no good would come of sending it, and so would not pain you unnecessarily.'

'O, no; I am indeed glad you have told me, Lord Luxellian. It is quite a mistaken kindness on their part. Is the review so much against me?' she inquired tremulously.

'No, no; not that exactly—though I almost forget its exact purport now. It was merely—merely sharp, you know— ungenerous, I might say. But really my memory does not enable me to speak decidedly.'

'We'll drive to the *Present* office, and get one directly; shall we, papa?'

'If you are so anxious, dear, we will, or send. But to-morrow will do.'

'And do oblige me in a little matter now, Miss Swancourt,' said Lord Luxellian warmly, and looking as if he were sorry he had brought news that disturbed her. 'I am in reality sent here as a special messenger by my little Polly and Katie to ask you to come into our carriage with them for a short time. I am just going to walk across into Piccadilly, and my wife is left alone with them. I am afraid they are rather spoilt children; but I have half promised them you shall come.'

The steps were let down, and Elfride was then transferred—to the intense delight of the little honourables, and to the great interest of well-dressed loungers with red skins and long necks, who curiously eyed the performance with their walking-sticks to their lips, occasionally laughing from far down their throats and with their eyes, their mouths not being concerned in the operation at all. Lord Luxellian then told the coachman to drive on, lifted his hat, smiled a smile that missed its mark and alighted on a total stranger, who bowed in bewilderment. Lord Luxellian looked long at Elfride.

The look was a manly, open, and genuine look of admiration; a momentary tribute of a kind which any honest Englishman might have paid to fairness without being ashamed of the feeling, or permitting it to encroach in the slightest degree upon his emotional obligations as a husband and head of a family. Then Lord Luxellian turned away, and walked musingly to the upper end of the promenade.

Mr. Swancourt had alighted at the same time with Elfride, crossing over to the Row for a few minutes to speak to a friend he recognised there; and his wife was thus left sole tenant of the carriage.

Now whilst this little act had been in course of performance, there stood among the promenading spectators a man of somewhat different description from the rest. Behind the general throng, in the rear of the chairs, and leaning against the trunk of a tree, he looked at Elfride with quiet and critical interest.

Three points about this unobtrusive person showed promptly to the exercised eye that he was not a Row man *pur sang*. First, an irrepressible wrinkle or two in the waist of his frock-coat—denoting that he had not damned his tailor sufficiently to drive that tradesman up to the orthodox high pressure of cunning workmanship. Second, a slight slovenliness of umbrella, occasioned by its owner's habit of resting heavily upon it, and using it as a veritable walking-stick, instead of letting its point touch the ground in the most coquettish of kisses, as is the proper Row manner to do. Third, and chief reason, that try how you might, you could scarcely help supposing, on looking at his face, that your eyes were not far from a well-finished mind, instead of the well-finished skin *et præterea nihil*, which is by rights the Mark of the Row.

The probability is that, had not Mrs. Swancourt been left alone in her carriage under the tree, this man would have remained in his unobserved seclusion. But seeing her thus, he came round to the front, stooped under the rail, and stood beside the carriage-door.

Mrs. Swancourt looked reflectively at him for a quarter of a minute, then held out her hand laughingly:

'Why, Henry Knight—of course it is! My—second—third—fourth cousin—what shall I say? At any rate, my kinsman.'

'Yes, one of a remnant not yet cut off. I scarcely was certain of you, either, from where I was standing.'

'I have not seen you since you first went to Oxford; consider the number of years! You know, I suppose, of my marriage?'

And there sprang up a dialogue concerning family matters of birth, death, and marriage, which it is not necessary to detail. Knight presently inquired:

'The young lady who changed into the other carriage is, then, your stepdaughter?'

'Yes, Elfride. You must know her.'

'And who was the lady in the carriage Elfride entered; who had an ill-defined and watery look, as if she were only the reflection of herself in a pool?'

'Lady Luxellian; very weakly, Elfride says. However, Henry, you'll come and see us, of course. 24 Chevron-square. Come this week. We shall only be in town a week or two longer.'

'Let me see. I am compelled to leave for Oxford to-morrow, where I shall be for several days; so that I must, I fear, lose the pleasure of seeing you in London this year.'

'Then come to Endelstow; why not return with us?'

'I am afraid if I were to come before August I should have to leave again in a day or two. I should be delighted to be with you at the beginning of that month; and I could stay a nice long time. I have thought of going westward all the summer.'

'Very well. Now remember that's a compact. And won't you wait now and see Mr. Swancourt? He will not be away ten minutes longer.'

'No; I'll beg to be excused; for I must get to my chambers again this evening before I go home; indeed I ought to have been there now—I have such a press of matters to attend to just at present. You will explain to him, please. Good-bye.'

'And let us know the day of your appearance as soon as you can.'

'I will.'

CHAPTER II.

'A WANDERING VOICE.'

Though sheer and intelligible griefs are not charmed away by being confided to mere acquaintances, the process is a palliative to certain ill-humours. A species of trouble which, like a stream, gets shallower by the simple operation of widening it in any quarter, is vexation that has for its chief ingredient perplexity.

On the evening of the day succeeding that of the meeting in the Park, Elfride and Mrs. Swancourt were engaged in conversation in the dressing-room of the latter. Such a treatment of such a case was in course of adoption here.

Elfride had just before received an affectionate letter from Stephen Smith in Bombay, which had been forwarded to her from Endelstow. But since this is not the case referred to, it is not worth while to pry farther into the contents of the letter than to discover that, with rash though pardonable confidence in coming times, he addressed her in high spirits as his darling future wife.

Probably there cannot be instanced a briefer and surer rule-of-thumb test of a man's temperament—sanguine or cautious than this: did he or does he ante-date the word wife in corresponding with a sweetheart he honestly loves?

She had taken this epistle into her own room, read a little of it, then *saved* the rest for to-morrow, not wishing to be so extravagant as to consume the pleasure all at once. Nevertheless, she could not resist the wish to enjoy yet a little more, so out came the letter again, and in spite of misgivings as to prodigality the whole was devoured. The letter was finally re-perused and placed in her pocket.

What was this? Also a newspaper for Elfride, which she had overlooked in her hurry to open the letter. It was the old number of the *Present*, containing the article upon her book, forwarded as had been requested.

Elfride had hastily read it through, shrunk perceptibly smaller, and had then gone with the paper in her hand to Mrs. Swancourt's dressing-room, to lighten or at least modify her vexation by a discriminating estimate from her stepmother.

She was now looking disconsolately out of the window.

'Never mind, my child,' said Mrs. Swancourt, after a careful perusal of the matter indicated. 'I don't see that the review is such a terrible one after all. Besides, everybody has forgotten about it by this time. I'm sure the opening is good enough for any book ever written. Just listen—it sounds better read aloud than when you pore over it silently: "*The Court of Kellyon Castle. A Romance of the Middle Ages. By Ernest Field.* In the belief that we were for a while escaping the monotonous repetition of wearisome details in modern social scenery, analyses of uninteresting character, or the unnatural unfoldings of a sensation plot, we took this volume into our hands with a feeling of pleasure. We were disposed to beguile ourselves with a fancy that some new change might possibly be rung upon donjon keeps, chain and plate armour, deeply-scarred cheeks, tender maidens disguised as pages, to which we had not listened long ago." Now that's a very good beginning in my opinion, and one to be proud of having brought out of a man who has never seen you.'

'Ah, yes,' murmured Elfride wofully. But, then, see farther on.'

'Well the next bit is rather unkind, I

must own,' said Mrs. Swancourt, and read on. ' " Instead of this we found ourselves in the hands of some young lady, hardly arrived at years of discretion, to judge by the silly device it has been thought worth while to adopt on the title-page, with the idea of disguising her sex." '

'I am not "silly"!' said Elfride indignantly. 'He might have called me anything but that.'

'You are not indeed. Well :—" Hands of a young lady ... whose chapters are simply devoted to impossible tournaments, towers, and escapades, which read like flat copies of like scenes in the stories of Mr. G. P. R. James, and the most unreal portions of *Ivanhoe*. The bait is so palpably artificial that the most credulous gudgeon turns away." Now, my dear, I don't see overmuch to complain of in that. It proves that you were clever enough to make him think of Sir Walter Scott, which is a great deal.'

'O yes; though I cannot romance myself, I am able to remind him of those who can.' Elfride intended to hurl these words sarcastically at her invisible enemy, but as she had no more satirical power than a wood-pigeon, they merely fell in a pretty murmur from lips shaped to a pout.

'Certainly: and that's something. Your book is good enough to be bad in an ordinary literary manner, and doesn't stand by itself in a melancholy position altogether worse than assailable.—"That interest in an historical romance may nowadays have any chance of being sustained, it is indispensable that the reader find himself under the guidance of some nearly extinct species of legendary, who, in addition to an impulse towards antiquarian research and an unweakened faith in the mediæval halo, shall possess an inventive faculty in which delicacy of sentiment is far overtopped by a power of welding to stirring incident a spirited variety of the elementary human passions." Well, that long-winded effusion doesn't refer to you at all, Elfride, merely something put in to fill up. Let me see, when does he come to you again; . . . not till the very end, actually. Here you are finally polished off:

'" But to return to the little work we have used as the text of this article. We are far from altogether disparaging the author's powers. She has a certain versatility that enables her to use with effect a style of narration peculiar to herself, which may be called a murmuring of delicate emotional trifles, the particular gift of those to whom the social sympathies of a peaceful time are as daily food. Hence, where matters of domiciliary experience, and the natural touches which make people real, can be introduced without anachronisms too striking, she is occasionally felicitous; and upon the whole we feel justified in saying that the book will bear looking into for the sake of those portions which have nothing whatever to do with the story."

'Well, I suppose it is intended for satire; but don't think anything more of it now, my dear. It is seven o'clock.' And Mrs. Swancourt rang for her maid.

Attack is more piquant than concord. Stephen's letter was concerning nothing but oneness with her: the review was the very reverse. And a stranger with neither name nor shape, age nor appearance, but a mighty voice, is naturally rather an interesting novelty to a lady he chooses to address. When Elfride fell asleep that night she was loving the writer of the letter, but thinking of the writer of that article.

CHAPTER III.

'THEN FANCY SHAPES—AS FANCY CAN.'

ON a day about three weeks later, the Swancourt trio were sitting quietly in the drawing-room of the Crags, Mrs. Swancourt's house at Endelstow, chatting, and taking easeful survey of their previous month or two of town—a tangible weariness even to people whose acquaintances there might be counted on the fingers.

A mere season in London with her practised stepmother had so advanced Elfride's perceptions, that her courtship by Stephen seemed emotionally meagre, and to have drifted back several years into a childish past. In regarding our mental experiences, as in visual observation, our own progress reads like a dwindling of that we progress from.

She was seated on a low chair, looking over her romance with melancholy interest for the first time since she had become acquainted with the remarks of the *Present* thereupon.

'Still thinking of that reviewer, Elfie?'

'Not of him personally; but I am thinking of his opinion. Really, on looking into the volume after this long time has elapsed, he seems to have estimated one part of it fairly enough.'

'No, no; I wouldn't show the white feather now! Fancy that of all people in the world the writer herself should go over to the enemy. How shall Monmouth's men fight when Monmouth runs away?'

'I don't do that. But I think he is right in some of his arguments, though wrong in others. And because he has some claim to my respect I regret all the more that he should think so mistakenly of my motives in one or two instances. It is more vexing to be misunderstood than to be misrepresented; and he misunderstands me. I cannot be easy whilst a person goes to rest night after night attributing to me intentions I never had.'

'He doesn't know your name, or anything about you. And he has doubtless forgotten there is such a book in existence by this time.'

'I myself should certainly like him to be put right upon one or two matters,' said the vicar, who had hitherto been silent. 'You see, critics go on writing, and are never corrected or argued with, and therefore are never improved.'

'Papa,' said Elfride brightening, 'write to him!'

'I would as soon write to him as look at him, for the matter of that,' said Mr. Swancourt.

'Do! And say, the young person who wrote the book did not adopt a masculine sobriquet in vanity or conceit, but because she was afraid it would be thought presumptuous to publish her name, and that she did not mean the story for such as he, but as a sweetener of history for young people, who might thereby acquire a taste for what went on in their own country hundreds of years ago, and be tempted to dive deeper into the subject. O, there is so much to explain; I wish I might write myself!'

'Now, Elfie, I'll tell you what we will do,' answered Mr. Swancourt, tickled with a sort of bucolic humour at the idea of criticising the critic. 'You shall write a clear account of what he is wrong in, and I will copy it and send it as mine.'

'Yes, now directly!' said Elfride, jumping up. 'When will you send it, papa?'

'O, in a day or two, I suppose,' he returned. Then the vicar paused and slightly yawned, and in the manner of elderly people, began to relax from his ardour for the undertaking now that it came to the point. 'But, really, it is hardly worth while.'

'O, papa!' said Elfride, with much disappointment. 'You said you would, and now you won't. That is not fair!'

'But how can we send it if we don't know whom to send it to?'

'If you really want to send such a thing, it can easily be done,' said Mrs. Swancourt, coming to her stepdaughter's rescue. 'An envelope addressed, "To the Critic of *The Court of Kellyon Castle*, care of the Editor of the *Present*," would find him.'

'Yes, I suppose it would.'

'Why not write your answer yourself, Elfride?' Mrs. Swancourt inquired.

'I might,' she said hesitatingly; 'and send it anonymously: that would be treating him as he has treated me.'

'No use in the world!'

'But I don't like to let him know my exact name. Suppose I put my initials only? The less you are known the more you are thought of.'

'Yes; you might do that.'

Elfride set to work there and then. Her one desire for the last fortnight seemed likely to be realised. As happens with sensitive and secluded minds, a continual dwelling upon the subject had magnified to colossal proportions the space she assumed herself to occupy or to have occupied in the occult critic's mind. At noon and at night she had been pestering herself with endeavours to perceive more distinctly his conception of her as a woman, apart from an authoress: whether he really despised her; whether he thought more or less of her than of ordinary young women who never ventured into the fire of criticism at all. Now she would have the satisfaction of feeling that at any rate he knew her true intent in crossing his path, and annoying him so by her performance, and be taught perhaps to despise it a little less.

Four days later an envelope, directed to Miss Swancourt, in a strange hand, made its appearance from the post-bag.

'O,' said Elfride, her heart sinking within her. 'Can it be from that man—a lecture for impertinence? And actually one for Mrs. Swancourt in the same handwriting!' She feared to open hers. 'Yet how can he know my name? No; it is somebody else.'

'Nonsense!' said her father grimly. 'You sent your initials, and the Directory was available. Though he wouldn't have taken the trouble to look there unless he had been thoroughly savage with you. I thought you wrote with rather more asperity than simple literary discussion required.' This timely clause was introduced to save the character of the vicar's judgment under any issue of affairs.

'Well, here I go,' said Elfride, desperately tearing open the seal.

'To be sure, of course,' exclaimed Mrs.

Swancourt; and looking up from her letter, 'Christopher, I quite forgot to tell you, when I mentioned that I had seen my distant relative, Harry Knight, that I invited him here for whatever length of time he could spare. And now he says he can come any day in August.'

'Write, and say the first of the month,' replied the indiscriminate vicar.

She read on. 'Goodness me—and that isn't all. He is actually the reviewer of Elfride's book. How absurd to be sure! I had no idea he reviewed novels or had anything to do with the *Present*. He is a barrister—and I thought he only wrote in the Quarterlies. Why, Elfride, you have brought about an odd entanglement! What does he say to you?'

Elfride had put down her letter with a dissatisfied flush on her face. 'I don't know. The idea of his knowing my name and all about me! .... Why, he says nothing particular, only this:—

'"My dear Madam,—Though I am sorry that my remarks should have seemed harsh, it is a pleasure to find that they have been the means of bringing forth such an ingeniously-argued reply. Unfortunately, it is so long since I wrote my paper, that my memory does not serve me sufficiently to say a single word in my defence, even supposing there remains one to be said, which is doubtful. You will find from a letter I have written to Mrs. Swancourt, that we are not such strangers to each other as we have been imagining. Possibly, I may have the pleasure of seeing you soon, when any argument you choose to advance shall receive all the attention it deserves."

'That is dim sarcasm—I know it is.'
'O, no, Elfride.'
'And then, his remarks didn't seem harsh—I mean I did not say so.'
'He thinks you are in a frightful tem-

per,' said Mr. Swancourt, chuckling in undertones.

'And he will come and see me, and find the authoress as contemptible in speech as she has been rude in manner. I do heartily wish I had never written a word to him.'

'Never mind,' said Mrs. Swancourt, also laughing in low quiet jerks; 'it will make the meeting such a comical affair, and afford splendid by-play for your father and myself. The idea of our running our heads against Harry Knight all the time! I cannot get over that.'

The vicar had immediately recognised the name, as that of Stephen Smith's preceptor and friend; but having ceased to concern himself in the matter, he made no remark to that effect, consistently forbearing to allude to anything which could restore recollection of their (to him) disagreeable mistakes with regard to poor Stephen's lineage and position. Elfride had of course perceived the same thing, which added to the complication of relationship, a mesh that her stepmother knew nothing of.

The identification scarcely heightened Knight's attractions now, though a twelvemonth ago she would only have cared to see him for the interest he possessed as Stephen's friend. Fortunately for Knight's advent, such a reason for welcome had only begun to be awkward to her at a time when the interest he had acquired on his own account made it no longer necessary.

These coincidences, in common with all relating to him, tended to keep Elfride's mind upon the stretch concerning Knight. As was her custom when upon the horns of a dilemma, she walked off by herself among the laurel-bushes, and there, standing still and splitting up a leaf without removing it from its stalk, fetched back recollections of Stephen's frequent words in praise of his friend, and wished she had listened more attentively. Then, still pulling the leaf, she would blush at some fancied mortification that would accrue to her from his words when they met, in consequence of her rudeness, as she now considered it, in writing to him.

The next development of her meditations was into the subject of what this man's personal appearance might be—was he tall or short, dark or fair, gay or grim? She would have asked Mrs. Swancourt, but for the risk she might thereby incur of some teasing remark being returned. Ultimately, Elfride would say, 'O, what a plague that reviewer is to me!' and turn her face to where she imagined India lay, and murmur to herself, 'Ah, my little husband, what are you doing now? Let me see, where are you—south, east, where? Behind that hill, ever so far behind!'

CHAPTER IV.

'HER WELCOME, SPOKE IN FALTERING PHRASE.'

'THERE is Henry Knight, I declare!' said Mrs. Swancourt one day.

They were gazing from the jutting angle of a wild enclosure not far from the Crags, which almost overhung the valley already described as leading up from the sea and little port of Stranton. The stony escarpment upon which they stood had the contour of a man's face, and it was covered with furze as with a beard. People in the field above were preserved from an accidental roll down these prominences and hollows by a hedge on the very crest, which was doing that kindly service for Elfride and her mother now.

Scrambling higher into the hedge and

stretching her neck farther over the furze, Elfride beheld the individual signified. He was walking leisurely along the little green path at the bottom, beside the stream, a satchel slung upon his left hip, a stout walking-stick in his hand, and a brown-holland sun-hat upon his head. The satchel was worn and old, and the outer polished surface of the leather was cracked and peeling off.

Knight having arrived over the hills to Stranton upon the top of a crazy omnibus, preferred to walk the remaining two miles up the valley, leaving his luggage to be brought on.

Behind him a boy wandered helter-skelter, and by that natural law of physics by which lesser bodies gravitate towards the greater, this boy drew near Knight, and trotted like a little dog close at his heels, whistling as he went, with his eyes fixed upon Knight's boots as they rose and fell.

When they had reached a point precisely opposite that in which Mrs. and Miss Swancourt lay in ambush, Knight stopped and turned round.

'Look here, my boy,' he said.

The boy parted his lips, opened his eyes, and answered nothing.

'Here's sixpence for you, on condition that you don't again come within twenty yards of my heels, all the way up the valley.'

The boy, who apparently had not known he had been looking at Knight's heels at all, took the sixpence mechanically, and Knight went on again, wrapt in meditation.

'A nice voice,' Elfride thought; 'but what a singular temper!'

'Now we must get indoors before he ascends the slope,' said Mrs. Swancourt softly. And they went across by a short cut over a stile, entering the lawn by a side door, and so on to the house.

Mr. Swancourt had gone into the village with the curate, and Elfride felt too nervous to await their visitor's arrival in the drawing-room with Mrs. Swancourt. So that when the elder lady entered, Elfride made some pretence of perceiving a new variety of crimson geranium, and lingered behind among the flower-beds.

There was nothing gained by this, after all, she thought; and a few minutes after boldly came into the house by the glass side-door. She walked along the corridor, and entered the drawing-room. Nobody was there.

A window at the angle of the room opened directly into an octagonal conservatory, enclosing the corner of the building. From the conservatory came voices in conversation—Mrs. Swancourt's and the stranger's.

She had expected him to talk brilliantly. To her surprise he was asking questions in quite a learner's manner, on subjects connected with the flowers and shrubs, that she had known for years. When after the lapse of a few minutes he spoke at some length, she considered there was a hard square decisiveness in the shape of his sentences, as if, unlike her own and Stephen's, they were not there and then newly constructed, but were drawn forth from a large store ready-made. They were now approaching the window to come in again.

'That is a flesh-coloured variety,' said Mrs. Swancourt. 'But oleanders, though they are such bulky shrubs, are so very easily wounded as to be unprunable—giants with the sensitiveness of young ladies. O, here is Elfride!'

Elfride looked as guilty and crestfallen as Lady Teazle at the fall of the screen. Mrs. Swancourt presented him half comically, and Knight in a minute or two seated himself beside the young lady.

A complexity of instincts checked Elfride's conventional smiles of complaisance and hospitality; and to make her still less comfortable, Mrs. Swancourt immediately afterwards left them together to seek her husband. Mr. Knight, however, did not seem at all incommoded by his feelings, and he said with light easefulness,

'So, Miss Swancourt, I have met you at last. You escaped me by a few minutes only when we were in London.'

'Yes. I found that you had seen Mrs. Swancourt.'

'And reviewer and reviewed are face to face at last,' he added unconcernedly.

'Yes: though the fact of your being a relative takes off the edge of it. It was strange that you should be one of Mrs. Swancourt's family all the time.' Elfride began to recover herself now, and to look into Knight's face. 'I was merely anxious to let you know my real meaning in writing the book—extremely anxious.'

'I can quite understand the wish; and I was gratified that my remarks should have reached home. They very seldom do, I am afraid.'

Elfride drew herself in. Here he was, sticking to his opinions as firmly as if friendship and politeness did not in the least require an immediate renunciation of them.

'You made me very uneasy and sorry by writing such things,' she murmured, suddenly dropping the mere *caqueterie* of a fashionable first introduction, and speaking with some of the dudgeon of a child towards a severe schoolmaster.

'That is rather the object of honest critics in such a case. Not to cause unnecessary sorrow: "To make you sorry after a proper manner, that ye may receive damage by us in nothing," as a powerful pen once wrote to the Gentiles. Are you going to write another romance?'

'Write another!' she said. 'That somebody may pen a condemnation and "nail't wi' Scripture" again, as you do now, Mr. Knight?'

'You may do better next time,' he said placidly: 'I think you will. But I would advise you to confine yourself to domestic scenes.'

'Thank you. But never again.'

'Well, you may be right. That a young lady has taken to writing is not by any means the best thing to hear about her.'

'What is the best?'

'I prefer not to say.'

'Do you know? Then do tell me, please.'

'To hear that she has married.'

Elfride hesitated. 'And what when she has been married?' she said at last, partly in order to withdraw her own person from the argument.

'Then to hear no more about her. It is as Smeaton said of his lighthouse: her greatest real praise, when the novelty of her inauguration has worn off, is that nothing happens to keep the talk of her alive.'

'Yes, I see,' said Elfride softly and thoughtfully. 'But of course it is different quite with men. Why don't you write novels, Mr. Knight?'

'Because I couldn't write one that would interest anybody.'

'Why?'

'For several reasons. It requires a talented omission of your real thoughts to make a novel popular, for one thing.'

'Is that really necessary? Well, I am sure you could learn to do that with practice,' said Elfride with an *ex-cathedrâ* air, as became a person who spoke from experience in the art. 'You would make a great name for certain,' she continued.

'So many people make a name nowadays, that it is more distinguished to remain in obscurity.'

'Tell me seriously—apart from the subject—why don't you write a volume instead of loose articles?' she insisted.

'Since you are pleased to make me talk

of myself, I will tell you seriously,' said Knight, not less amused by this catechism by his young friend than he was interested in her appearance. 'As I have implied, I have not the wish. And if I had the wish, I could not now concentrate sufficiently. We all have only our one cruse of energy given us to make the best of. And where that energy has been leaked away week by week, quarter by quarter, as mine has for the last nine or ten years, there is not enough dammed back behind the mill at any given period to supply the quantum a complete book on any subject requires. Then there is the self-confidence and waiting power. Where quick results have grown customary, they are fatal to a lively faith in the future.'

'Yes, I comprehend; and so you choose to write in fragments?'

'No, I don't choose to do it in the sense you mean; choosing from a whole world of professions, all possible. It was by the constraint of accident merely. Not that I object to the accident.'

'Why don't you object — I mean, why do you feel so quiet about things?' Elfride was half afraid to question him so, but her intense curiosity to see what the inside of literary Mr. Knight was like, kept her going on. Knight certainly did not mind being frank with her. Instances of this trait in men who have warm feelings, but are reticent from habit, may be recalled by all of us. When they find a listener who can by no possibility make use of them, rival them, or condemn them, reserved and even suspicious men of the world become frank, keenly enjoying the inner side of their frankness.

'Why I don't mind the accidental constraint,' he replied, 'is because, in making beginnings, a chance limitation of direction is often better than absolute freedom.'

'I see—that is, I should if I quite understood what all those generalities mean.'

'Why, this: That an arbitrary foundation for one's work, which no length of thought can alter, leaves the attention free to fix itself on the work itself, and make the best of it.'

'Lateral compression forcing altitude, as would be said in that tongue,' she said mischievously. 'And I suppose where no limit exists, as in the case of a rich man with a wide taste who wants to do something, it will be better to choose a limit capriciously than to have none.'

'Yes,' he said meditatively. 'I can go as far as that.'

'Well,' resumed Elfride, 'I think it better for a man's nature if he does nothing in particular.'

'There is such a case as being obliged to.'

'Yes, yes; I was speaking of when you are not obliged to for any other reason than delight in the prospect of fame. I have thought many times lately that a thin widespread happiness, commencing now, and of a piece with the days of your life, is preferable to an anticipated heap far away in the future, and none now.'

'Why that's the very thing I said just now as being the principle of all ephemeral doers like myself.'

'O, I am sorry to have parodied you,' she said, with some confusion. 'Yes, of course. That is what you meant about not trying to be famous.' And she added, with the quickness of conviction characteristic of her mind: 'There is much littleness in trying to be great. A man must think a good deal of himself, and be conceited enough to believe in himself, before he tries at all.'

'But it is soon enough to say there is harm in a man's thinking a good deal of himself when it is proved he has been thinking wrong, and too soon then sometimes. Besides, we should not conclude that a man who strives earnestly for success does so with a strong sense of his own merit. He may see how little success has to do with merit, and his motive may be his very humility.'

This manner of treating her rather provoked Elfride. No sooner did she agree with him than he ceased to seem to wish it, and took the other side. 'Ah,' she thought inwardly, 'I shall have nothing to do with a man of this kind, though he is our visitor.'

'I think you will find,' resumed Knight, pursuing the conversation more for the sake of finishing off his thoughts on the subject than for engaging her attention, 'that in actual life it is merely a matter of instinct with men—this trying to push on. They awake to a recognition that they have, without premeditation, begun to try a little, and they say to themselves, "Since I have tried thus much, I will try a little more." They go on because they have begun.'

Elfride, in her turn, was not particularly attending to his words at this moment. She had, unconsciously to herself, a way of seizing any point in the remarks of an interlocutor which interested her, and dwelling upon it, and thinking thoughts of her own thereupon, totally oblivious of all that he might say in continuation. On such occasions she artlessly surveyed the person speaking, and then there was a time for a painter. Her eyes seemed to look at you, and past you, as you were then, into your future; and past your future into your eternity—not reading it, but gazing in an unused, unconscious way — her mind still clinging to its original thought.

This is how she was looking at Knight.

Suddenly Elfride became conscious of what she was doing, and was painfully confused.

'What were you so intent upon in me?' he inquired.

'As far as I was thinking of you at

all, I was thinking how clever you are,' she said, with a want of premeditation that was startling in its honesty and simplicity.

Feeling restless now that she had so unwittingly spoken, she arose and stepped to the window, having heard the voices of her father and Mrs. Swancourt coming up below the terrace. 'Here they are,' she said, going out. Knight walked out upon the lawn behind her. She stood upon the edge of the terrace, close to the stone balustrade, and looked towards the sun, hanging over a glade, just now fair as Tempe's vale, up which her father was walking.

Knight could not help looking at her. The sun was within ten degrees of the horizon, and its yellow light flooded her face and heightened the bright rose colour of her cheeks to a vermilion red, their moderate pink hue being only seen in its natural tone where the cheek curved round into shadow. The ends of her hanging hair softly dragged themselves backwards and forwards upon her shoulder as each faint breeze thrust against or relinquished it. Fringes and ribbons of her dress, moved by the same breeze, licked like tongues upon the parts around them, and fluttering forward from shady folds caught likewise their share of the lustrous orange glow.

Mr. Swancourt shouted out a welcome to Knight from a distance of about thirty yards, and after a few preliminary words proceeded to a conversation of deep earnestness on Knight's fine old family name, and theories as to lineage and intermarriage connected therewith. Knight's portmanteau having in the mean time arrived, they soon retired to prepare for dinner, which had been postponed two hours later than the usual time of that meal.

An arrival was an event in the life of Elfride, now that they were again in the country, and that of Knight necessarily an engrossing one. And that evening she went to bed for the first time without thinking of Stephen at all.

CHAPTER V.

'HE HEARD HER MUSICAL PANTS.'

THE old tower of West Endelstow Church had reached the last weeks of its existence. It was to be replaced by a new one. Planks and poles had arrived in the churchyard, iron bars had been thrust into the venerable crack extending down the belfry wall to the foundation, the bells had been taken down, the owls had forsaken this home of their forefathers, and six iconoclasts in white fustian, to whom a cracked edifice was a species of Mumbo Jumbo, had taken lodgings in the village previous to commencing the actual removal of the stones.

This was the day after Knight's arrival. To enjoy for the last time the prospect seaward from the summit, the vicar, Mrs.

Swancourt, Knight, and Elfride, all ascended the winding turret—Mr. Swancourt stepping forward with many loud pants, his wife struggling along silently, but suffering none the less. They had hardly reached the top when a large lurid cloud, palpably a reservoir of rain, thunder, and lightning was seen to be advancing overhead from the north.

The two cautious elders suggested an immediate return, and proceeded to put it in practice as regarded themselves.

'Dear me, I wish I had not come up,' exclaimed Mrs. Swancourt.

'We shall be slower than you two in going down,' the vicar said over his shoulder, 'and so, don't you start till we are nearly at the bottom, or you will run over us and break our necks somewhere in the darkness of the turret.'

Accordingly Elfride and Knight waited on the leads till the staircase should be clear. Knight was not in a talkative mood that morning. Elfride was rather wilful, by reason of his inattention, which she privately set down to his thinking her not worth talking to. Whilst Knight stood watching the rise of the cloud, she sauntered to the other side of the tower, and there remembered a giddy feat she had performed the year before. It was to walk round upon the parapet of the tower—which was quite without battlement or pinnacle, and presented a smooth flat surface about two feet wide, forming a pathway on all the four sides. Without reflecting in the least upon what she was doing, she now stepped upon the parapet in the old way, and began walking along.

'We are down, cousin Henry,' cried Mrs. Swancourt up the turret. 'Follow us when you like.'

Knight turned and saw Elfride commencing her elevated promenade. His face flushed with mingled concern and anger at her rashness.

'I certainly gave you credit for more common sense,' he said.

She reddened a little and walked on.

'Miss Swancourt, I insist upon your coming down,' he exclaimed.

'I will in a minute. I am safe enough. I have done it often.'

At that moment, by reason of a slight perturbation his words had caused in her, Elfride's foot caught itself in a little tuft of grass growing in a joint of the stonework, and she almost lost her balance. Knight sprang forward with a face of horror. By what seemed the special interposition of a considerate Providence she tottered to the inner edge of the parapet instead of to the outer, and reeled over upon the lead roof two or three feet below the wall.

Knight seized her as in a vice, and he said, panting, 'That ever I should have met a woman fool enough to do a thing of that kind! Good God, you ought to be ashamed of yourself!'

The close proximity of the Shadow of Death had made her sick and pale as a corpse before he spoke. Already lowered to that state, his words completely overpowered her, and she swooned away as he held her.

Elfride's eyes were not closed for more than forty seconds. She opened them, and remembered the position instantly. His face had altered its expression from stern anger to pity. But his severe remarks had rather frightened her, and she struggled to be free.

'If you can stand, of course you may,' he said, and loosened his arms. 'I hardly know whether most to laugh at your freak or to chide for its folly.'

She immediately sank upon the leadwork. Knight lifted her again. 'Are you hurt?' he said.

She murmured an incoherent expression, and tried to smile; saying, with a fitful aversion of her face, 'I am only frightened. Put me down, do put me down!'

'But you can't walk,' said Knight.

'You don't know that; how can you? I am only frightened, I tell you,' she answered petulantly, and raised her hand to her forehead. Knight then saw that she was bleeding from a severe cut in her wrist, apparently where it had descended upon a salient corner of the leadwork. Elfride too seemed to perceive and feel this, now for the first time, and for a minute nearly lost consciousness again. Knight rapidly bound his handkerchief round the place, and to add to the complication, the thundercloud he had been watching began to shed some heavy drops of rain. Knight looked up and saw the vicar striding towards the house, and Mrs. Swancourt waddling beside him, like a hard-driven duck.

'As you are so faint, it will be much better to let me carry you down,' said Knight; 'or at any rate inside out of the rain.' But her objection to be lifted made it impossible for him to support her for more than five steps.

'This is folly, great folly,' he exclaimed, setting her down.

'Indeed!' she murmured, with tears in her eyes. 'I say I will not be carried, and you say this is folly.'

'So it is.'

'No, it isn't.'

'It is folly, I think. At any rate the origin of it all is.'

'I don't agree to it. And you needn't get so angry with me; I am not worth it.'

'Indeed you are. You are worth the enmity of princes, as was said of such another. Now, then, will you clasp your hands behind my neck, that I may carry you down without hurting you?'

'No, no.'

'You had better, or I shall foreclose.'

'What's that?'

'Deprive you of your chance.'

Elfride gave a little toss.

'Now, don't writhe so when I attempt to carry you.'

'I can't help it.'

'Then submit quietly.'

'I don't care, I don't care,' she murmured in languid tones and with closed eyes.

He took her into his arms, entered the turret, and with slow and cautious steps descended round and round. Then, with the gentleness of a nursing mother, he attended to the cut on her arm. During his progress through the operations of wiping it and binding it up anew, her face changed its aspect from pained indifference to something like bashful interest, interspersed with small tremors and shudders of a trifling kind.

In the centre of each pale cheek a small red spot the size of a wafer had now made its appearance, and continued to grow larger. Elfride momentarily expected a recurrence to the lecture on her foolishness, but Knight said no more than this,

'Promise me *never* to walk on that parapet again.'

'It will be pulled down soon: so I do.' In a few minutes she continued in a lower tone, and seriously, 'You are familiar of course, as everybody is, with those strange sensations we sometimes have, that our life for the moment exists in duplicate.'

'That we have lived through that moment before?'

'Or shall again. Well, I felt on the tower that something similar to that scene is again to be common to us both.'

'God forbid!' said Knight. 'Promise me that you will never again walk on any such place on any consideration.'

'I do.'

'That such a thing has not been before, we know. That it shall not be again, you vow. Therefore think no more of such a foolish fancy.'

There had fallen a great deal of rain, but unaccompanied by lightning. A few minutes longer, and the storm had ceased.

'Now, take my arm, please.'

'O, no, it is not necessary.' This relapse into wilfulness was because he had again connected the epithet foolish with her.

'Nonsense: it is quite necessary; it will rain again directly, and you are not half recovered.' And without more ado, Knight took her hand, drew it under his arm, and held it there so firmly that she could not have removed it without a struggle. Feeling, at thus being led along, like a colt in a halter for the first time, yet afraid to be angry, it was to her great relief that she saw the carriage coming round the corner to fetch them.

Her fall upon the roof was necessarily explained to some extent upon their entering the house; but both forbore to mention a word of what she had been doing to cause such an accident. During the remainder of the afternoon Elfride was invisible; but at dinner-time she appeared as bright as ever.

In the drawing-room, after having been exclusively engaged with Mr. and Mrs. Swancourt through the intervening hour, Knight again found himself thrown with Elfride. She had been looking over a chess problem in one of the illustrated periodicals.

'You like chess, Miss Swancourt?'

'Yes. It is my favourite scientific game; indeed, excludes every other. Do you play?'

'I have played; though not lately.'

'Challenge him, Elfride,' said the vicar heartily. 'She plays very well for a lady, Mr. Knight.'

'Shall we play?' asked Elfride tentatively.

'O, certainly. I shall be delighted.'

The game began. Mr. Swancourt had

forgotten a similar performance with Stephen Smith the year before. Elfride had not; but she had begun to take for her maxim the undoubted truth that the necessity of continuing faithful to Stephen without suspicion, dictated a fickle behaviour almost as imperatively as fickleness itself; a fact, however, which would give a startling advantage to the latter quality, should it ever appear.

Knight, by one of those inexcusable oversights which will sometimes afflict the best of players, placed his rook in the arms of one of her pawns. It was her first advantage. She looked triumphant — even ruthless.

'By George! what was I thinking of?' said Knight quietly; and then relinquished concern at his accident.

'Club laws we'll have, won't we, Mr. Knight?' said Elfride suasively.

'O, yes, certainly,' said Mr. Knight, thought however just occurring to his mind that he had two or three times allowed her to replace a man, on her religiously assuring him that such a move was an absolute blunder.

She immediately took up the unfortunate rook and the contest proceeded, Elfride having now rather the better of the game. Then he won the exchange, regained his position, and began to press her hard. Elfride grew flurried, and placed her queen on his remaining rook's file.

'There—how stupid! Upon my word, I did not see your rook. Of course nobody but a fool would have put a queen there knowingly.'

She spoke excitedly, half expecting her antagonist to give her back the move.

'Nobody, of course,' said Knight serenely, and stretched out his hand towards his royal victim.

'It is not very pleasant to have it taken advantage of, then,' she said with some vexation.

'Club laws, I think you said?' returned Knight blandly, and mercilessly appropriating the queen.

She was on the brink of pouting, but was ashamed to show it; tears almost stood in her eyes. She had been trying so hard —so very hard—thinking and thinking till her brain was in a whirl; and it seemed so heartless of him to treat her so, after all.

'I think it is—' she began.

'What?'

'—Unkind to take advantage of a pure mistake I make in that way.'

'I lost my rook by even a purer mistake,' said the enemy, in an inexorable tone, without lifting his eyes.

'Yes, but—' However, as his logic was absolutely unanswerable, she merely registered a protest. 'I cannot endure those cold-blooded ways of clubs and professional players, like Staunton and Morphy. Just as if it really mattered whether you have raised your fingers from a man or no.'

Knight smiled as pitilessly as before, and they went on in silence.

'Checkmate,' said Knight.

'Another game,' said Elfride, peremptorily; and looking very warm.

'With all my heart,' said Knight.

'Checkmate,' said Knight again, at the end of forty minutes.

'Another game,' she returned resolutely.

'I'll give you the odds of a bishop,' Knight said to her kindly.

'No, thank you,' Elfride replied, in a tone intended for courteous indifference; but, as a fact, very cavalier indeed.

'Checkmate,' said her opponent, without the least emotion.

Elfride, the difference between your condition of mind now, and when you purposely made blunders that Stephen Smith might win!

It was bed-time. Her mind as if it would throb itself out of her head, she went off to her chamber, full of mortification at being beaten time after time when she herself was the aggressor. Having for two or three years enjoyed the reputation throughout the globe of her father's brain— which almost constituted her entire world —of being an excellent player, this fiasco was intolerable; for unfortunately the person most dogged in the belief in a false reputation is always that one, the possessor, who has the best means of knowing that it is not true.

In bed no sleep came to soothe her; that gentle thing being the very middle-of-summer friend in this respect of flying away at the merest troublous cloud. After lying awake till two o'clock, an idea seemed to strike her. She softly arose, got a light, and fetched a Chess Praxis from the library. Returning and sitting up in bed, she diligently studied the volume till the clock struck five, and her eyelids felt thick and heavy. She then extinguished the light and lay down again.

'You look pale, Elfride,' said Mrs. Swancourt the next morning at breakfast. 'Isn't she, cousin Harry?'

A young lady who is scarcely ill at all can hardly help becoming so when regarded as such by all eyes turning upon her at the table in obedience to some remark. Everybody looked at Elfride. She certainly was pale.

'Am I pale?' she said with a faint smile. 'I did not sleep much. I could not get rid of armies of bishops and knights, try how I would.'

'Chess is a bad thing just before bedtime; especially for excitable people like yourself, dear. Don't ever play late again.'

'I'll play early instead. Cousin Knight,' she said in imitation of Mrs. Swancourt, 'will you oblige me in something?'

'Even to half my kingdom.'

'Well, it is to play one game more.'

'When?'

'Now, instantly; the moment we have breakfasted.'

'Nonsense, Elfride,' said her father. 'Making yourself a slave to the game like that.'

'But I want to, papa. Honestly, I am restless at having been so ignominiously overcome. And Mr. Knight doesn't mind. So what harm can there be?'

'Let us play by all means, if you wish it,' said Knight.

So when breakfast was over, the combatants withdrew to the quiet of the library, and the door was closed. Elfride seemed to have an idea that her conduct was rather ill-regulated, and startlingly free from conventional restraint. And worse, she fancied upon Knight's face a slightly amused look at her proceedings.

'You think me foolish, I suppose,' she said recklessly; 'but I want to do my very best just once, and see whether I can overcome you.'

'Certainly: nothing more natural. Though I am afraid it is not the plan adopted by women of the world after a defeat.'

'Why, pray?'

'Because they know that as good as overcoming is skill in effacing recollection of being overcome, and turn their attention to that entirely.'

'I am wrong again, of course.'

'Perhaps your wrong is more pleasing than their right.'

'I don't quite know whether you mean that, or whether you are laughing at me,' she said, looking doubtingly at him, yet inclining to accept the more flattering interpretation. 'I am almost sure you think it vanity in me to think I am a match for you. Well, if you do, I say that vanity is no crime in such a case.'

'Well, perhaps not. Though it is hardly a virtue.'

'O, yes, in battle. Nelson's bravery lay in his vanity.'

'Indeed! Then so did his death.'

'O, no, no! For it is written in the book of the prophet Shakespeare,

"Fear and be slain? no worse can come to fight;
And fight and die, is death destroying death!"'

And down they sat, and the contest began, Elfride having the first move. The game progressed. Elfride's heart beat so violently that she could not sit still. Her dread was lest he should hear it. And he did discover it at last—some flowers upon the table being set throbbing by its pulsations.

'I think we had better give over,' said Knight, looking at her gently. 'It is too much for you, I know. Let us write down the position, and finish another time.'

'No, please not,' she implored. 'I should not rest if I did not know the result at once. It is your move.'

Ten minutes passed.

She started up suddenly. 'I know what you are doing!' she cried; an angry colour upon her cheeks, and her eyes indignant. 'You were thinking of letting me win to please me!'

'I don't mind owning that I was,' Knight responded phlegmatically, and appearing all the more so by contrast with her own turmoil.

'But you must not! I won't have it.'

'Very well.'

'No, that will not do; I insist that you promise not to do any such absurd thing. It is insulting me!'

'Very well, madam. I won't do any such absurd thing. You shall not win.'

'That is to be proved,' she returned proudly; and the play went on.

Nothing is now heard but the ticking of a quaint old timepiece on the summit of a bookcase. Ten minutes pass; he captures her knight; she takes his knight, and looks a very Rhadamanthus.

More minutes tick away: she takes his pawn and has the advantage, showing her sense of it rather prominently.

Five minutes more: he takes her bishop: she brings things even by taking his knight.

Three minutes: she looks bold, and takes his queen: he looks placid, and takes hers.

Eight or ten minutes pass: he takes a pawn: she utters a little pooh! but not the ghost of a pawn can she take in retaliation.

Ten minutes pass: he takes another pawn and says, 'Check!' She flushes, extricates herself by capturing his bishop, and looks triumphant. He immediately takes her bishop: she looks surprised.

Five minutes longer: she makes a dash and takes his only remaining bishop; he replies by taking her only remaining knight.

Two minutes: he gives check; her mind is now in a painful state of tension, and she shades her face with her hand.

Yet a few minutes more: he takes her

rook and checks again. She literally trembles now lest an artful surprise she has in store for him shall be anticipated by the surprise he evidently has in store for her.

Five minutes: 'Checkmate in two moves!' exclaims Elfride.

'If you can,' says Knight.

'O, I have miscalculated; that is cruel!'

'Checkmate,' says Knight; and the victory is won.

Elfride arose and turned away without letting him see her face. Once in the hall she ran up-stairs and into her room, and flung herself down upon her bed, weeping bitterly.

'Where is Elfride?' said her father at luncheon.

Knight listened anxiously for the answer. He had been hoping to see her again before this time.

'She isn't well, sir,' was the reply.

Mrs. Swancourt arose and left the room, going up-stairs to Elfride's apartment.

At the door was Unity, who occupied in the new establishment a position between young-lady's maid and middle-housemaid.

'She is sound asleep, ma'am,' Unity whispered.

Mrs. Swancourt opened the door. Elfride was lying full-dressed on the bed, her face hot and red, her arms thrown abroad. At intervals of a minute she tossed restlessly from side to side, and indistinctly moaned words used in the game of chess.

Mrs. Swancourt had a turn for doctoring, and felt her pulse. It was twanging like a harp-string, at the rate of nearly two hundred a minute. Softly moving the sleeping girl to a little less cramped position, she went down-stairs again.

'She is asleep now,' said Mrs. Swancourt. 'She does not seem very well. Cousin Knight, what were you thinking of? her tender brain won't bear cudgelling like your great head. You should have strictly forbidden her to play again.'

In truth, the essayist's experience of the nature of young women was far less extensive than his abstract knowledge of them led himself and others to believe. He could pack them into sentences like a workman, but empirically was nowhere.

'I am indeed sorry,' said Knight, feeling even more than he expressed. 'But surely, the young lady knows best what is good for her?'

'Bless you, that's just what she doesn't know. She never thinks of such things, does she, Christopher? Her father and I have to command her and keep her in order, as you would a child. She will say things worthy of a French epigrammatist, and act like a robin in a greenhouse. But I think we will send for Dr. Granson—there can be no harm.'

A man was straightway dispatched on horseback to Stranton, and the gentleman known as Dr. Granson came in the course of the afternoon. He pronounced her nervous system to be in a decided state of disorder; forwarded some soothing draught, and gave orders that on no account whatever was she to play chess again.

The next morning Knight waited with a curiously compounded feeling for her entry to breakfast. The female servants came in to prayers at irregular intervals, and as each entered, he could not, to save his life, avoid turning his head with the hope that she might be Elfride. Mr. Swancourt began reading without waiting for her. Then somebody glided in noiselessly; Knight softly glanced up: it was only the little kitchen-maid. Knight thought reading prayers a bore.

He went out alone, and for almost the first time failed to recognise that holding converse with Nature's charms was not solitude. On nearing the house again he perceived his young friend crossing a slope by a path which ran into the one he was following, in the angle of the field. Here they met. Elfride was at once exultant and abashed: coming into his presence had upon her the effect of entering a cathedral.

Knight had his note-book in his hand, and had, in fact, been in the very act of writing therein, when they came in view of each other. He left off in the midst of a sentence, and proceeded to inquire warmly concerning her state of health. She said she was perfectly well, and indeed had never looked better. Her health was as inconsequent as her actions. Her lips were red, *without* the polish that cherries have, and their redness margined with the white skin in a clearly-defined line, which had nothing of jagged confusion in it. Altogether she stood as the last person in the world to be knocked over by a game of chess, because too ephemeral-looking to play one.

'Are you taking notes?' she inquired with an alacrity plainly arising less from interest in the subject than from a wish to divert his thoughts from her body.

'Yes; I was making an entry. And with your permission I will complete it.' Knight then stood still, and wrote. Elfride remained beside him a moment, and afterwards walked on.

'I should like to see all the secrets that are in that book,' she gaily flung back to him over her shoulder.

'I don't think you would find much to interest you.'

'I know I should.'

'Then of course I have no more to say.'

'But I would ask this question first. Is it a book of mere facts concerning journeys and expenditure, and so on, or a book of thoughts?'

'Well, to tell the truth, it is not exactly either. It consists for the most part of jottings for articles and essays, disjointed and disconnected, of no possible interest to anybody but myself.'

'It contains, I suppose, your developed thoughts in embryo?'

'Yes.'

'If they are interesting when enlarged to the size of an article, what must they be in their concentrated form? Pure rectified spirit, above proof; before it is lowered to be fit for human consumption: "words that burn" indeed.'

'Rather like a balloon before it is inflated: flabby, shapeless, dead. You could hardly read them.'

'May I try?' she said coaxingly, 'I wrote my poor romance in that way—I mean in bits, out of doors—and I should like to see whether your way of entering things is the same as mine.'

'Really, that's rather an awkward request. I suppose I can hardly refuse now you have asked so directly; but—'

'You think me ill-mannered in asking. But does not this justify me—your writing in my presence, Mr. Knight? If I had lighted upon your book by chance, it would have been different; but you stand before me, and say, " excuse me," without caring whether I do or not, and write on, and then tell me they are not private facts but public ideas.'

'Very well, Miss Swancourt. If you really must see, the consequences be upon your own head. Remember, my advice to you is to leave my book alone.'

'But with that caution I have your permission?'

'Yes.'

She hesitated a moment, looked at his hand containing the book, then laughed, and saying, 'I must see it,' withdrew it from his fingers.

Knight rambled on towards the house, leaving her standing in the path turning over the leaves. By the time he had reached the wicket-gate he saw that she had moved, and waited till she came up.

Elfride had closed the note-book, and

was carrying it disdainfully by the corner between her finger and thumb; her face wore a nettled look. She silently extended the volume towards him, raising her eyes no higher than her hand was lifted.

'Take it,' said Elfride quickly. 'I don't want to read it.'

'Could you understand it?' said Knight.

'As far as I looked. But I didn't care to read much.'

'Why, Miss Swancourt?'

'Only because I didn't wish to—that's all.'

'I warned you that you might not.'

'Yes, but I never supposed you would have put *me* there.'

'Your name is not mentioned once within the four corners.'

'Not my name—I know that.'

'Nor your description, nor anything by which anybody would recognise you.'

'Except myself. For what is this?' she exclaimed, taking it from him and opening a page. 'August 7. That's the day before yesterday. But I won't read it,' Elfride said, closing the book again with pretty hauteur. 'Why should I? I had no business to ask to see your book, and it serves me right.'

Knight hardly recollected what he had written, and turned over the book to see. He came to this:

'Aug. 7. Girl gets into her teens, and her self-consciousness is born. After a certain interval passed in infantine helplessness, it begins to act. Simple, young, and inexperienced at first. Persons of observation can tell to a nicety how old this consciousness is by the skill it has acquired in the art necessary to its success—the art of hiding itself. Generally begins career by actions which are popularly termed showing-off. Method adopted depends in each case upon the disposition, rank, residence, of the young lady attempting it. Town-bred girl will utter some moral paradox on fast men, or love. Country Miss adopts the more material media of taking a ghastly fence, whistling, or making your blood run cold by appearing to risk her neck. (*Mem.* On Endelstow tower.)

'An innocent vanity is of course the origin of these displays. "Look at me," say these youthful beginners in womanly artifice, without reflecting whether or not it be to their advantage to show so very much of themselves. (Amplify and correct for paper on Artless Arts.)'

'Yes, I remember now,' said Knight. 'The notes were certainly suggested by your manœuvre on the church tower. But you must not think too much of such random observations,' he continued encouragingly, as he noticed her injured looks. 'A mere fancy passing through my head assumes a factitious importance to you, because it has been made permanent by being written down. All mankind think thoughts as bad as those of people they most love on earth, but such thoughts never getting embodied on paper, it becomes assumed that they never existed. I daresay that you yourself have thought some disagreeable thing or other of me, which would seem just as bad as this if written. I challenge you, now, to tell me.'

'The worst thing I have thought of you?'

'Yes.'

'I must not.'

'O, yes.'

'I thought you were rather round-shouldered.'

Knight looked slightly redder.

'And that there was a little bald spot on the top of your head.'

'Heh-heh! Two ineradicable defects,' said Knight, there being a faint ghastliness discernible in his laugh. 'They are much worse in a lady's eye than being thought self-conscious, I suppose.'

'Ah, that's very fine,' she said, too inexperienced to perceive her hit, and hence not quite disposed to forgive his notes. 'You alluded to me in that entry as if I were such a child, too. Everybody does that. I cannot understand it. I am quite a woman, you know. How old do you think I am?'

'How old? Why, seventeen, I should say. All girls are seventeen.'

'You are wrong. I am nearly nineteen. Which class of women do you like best, those who seem younger, or those who seem older than they are?'

'Off-hand I should be inclined to say those who seem older.'

So it was not Elfride's class.

'But it is well known,' she said eagerly, and there was something touching in the artless anxiety to be thought much of she revealed by her words, 'that the slower a nature is to develop, the richer the nature. Youths and girls who are men and women before they come of age are nobodies by the time backward people have shown their full compass.'

'Yes,' said Knight thoughtfully. 'There is really something in that remark. But at the risk of offence I must remind you that you there take it for granted that the woman behind her time at a given age has not reached the end of her tether. Her backwardness may be not because she is slow to develop, but because she soon exhausted her capacity for developing.'

Elfride looked disappointed. By this time they were indoors. Mrs. Swancourt, to whom match-making by any honest means was meat and drink, had now a little scheme of that nature concerning this pair. The morning-room, in which they both expected to find her, was empty; the old lady having, for the above reason, vacated it by the second door as they entered by the first.

Knight went to the chimneypiece, and carelessly surveyed two portraits on ivory.

'Though these pink ladies had very rudimentary features, judging by what I see here,' he observed, 'they had unquestionably beautiful heads of hair.'

'Yes; and that is everything,' said Elfride, possibly conscious of her own, possibly not.

'Not everything; though a great deal, certainly.'

'Which colour do you like best?' she ventured to ask.

'More depends on its abundance than on its colour.'

'Abundances being equal, may I inquire your favourite colour?'

'Dark.'

'I mean for women,' she said with the minutest fall of countenance, and a hope that she had been misunderstood.

'So do I,' Knight replied.

It was impossible for any man not to know the colour of Elfride's hair. In women who wear it plainly such a feature may be overlooked by men not given to ocular intentness. But hers was always in the way. You saw her hair as far as you could see her sex, and knew that it was the palest brown. She knew instantly that Knight, being perfectly aware of this, had an independent standard of admiration in the matter.

Elfride was thoroughly vexed. She could not but be struck with the honesty of his opinions, and the worst of it was, that the more they went against her, the more she respected them. And now, like a reckless gambler, she hazarded her last and best treasure. Her eyes: they were her all now.

'What coloured eyes do you like best, Mr. Knight?' she said slowly.

'Honestly, or as a compliment?'

'Of course honestly; I don't want anybody's compliment.'

And yet Elfride knew otherwise: that a compliment or word of approval from that man then would have been like a well to a famished Arab.

'I prefer hazel,' he said serenely.

She had played and lost again.

CHAPTER VI.

'LOVE WAS IN THE NEXT DEGREE.'

KNIGHT had none of those light familiarities of speech which, by judicious touches of epigrammatic flattery, obliterate a woman's recollection of the speaker's abstract opinions. So no more was said by either on the subject of hair, eyes, or development. Elfride's mind had been impregnated with sentiments of her own smallness to an uncomfortable degree of distinctness, and her discomfort was visible in her face. The whole tendency of the conversation latterly had been to quietly but surely disparage her; and she was fain to take Stephen into favour in self-defence. He would not have been so unloving, she said, as to admire an idiosyncrasy and features different from her own. True, Stephen had declared he loved her: Mr. Knight had never done anything of the sort. Somehow this did not mend matters, and the sensation of her smallness in Knight's eyes still remained. Had the position been reversed—had Stephen loved her in spite of a differing taste, and had Knight been indifferent in spite of her resemblance to his ideal, it would have engendered far happier thoughts. As matters stood, Stephen's admiration might have its root in a blindness the result of passion. Perhaps any keen man's judgment was condemnatory of her.

During the remainder of Saturday they were more or less thrown with their seniors, and no conversation arose which was exclusively their own. When Elfride was in bed that night her thoughts recurred to the same subject. At one moment she insisted that it was ill-natured of him to speak so decisively as he had done; the next, that it was sterling honesty.

'Ah, what a poor nobody I am!' she said, sighing. 'People like him, who go about the great world, don't care in the least what I am like either in mood or feature.'

Perhaps a man who has got thoroughly into a woman's mind in this manner, is half-way to her heart; for the distance between her reason and her feeling is proverbially short.

'And are you really going away this week?' said Mrs. Swancourt to Knight on the following evening, which was Sunday.

They were all leisurely climbing the hill to the church, where a last service was now to be held at the rather exceptional time of evening instead of in the afternoon, previous to the demolition of the ruinous portions.

'I am intending to cross to Cork from Bristol,' returned Knight; 'and then I go on to Dublin.'

'Return this way, and stay a little longer with us,' said the vicar. 'A week is nothing. We have hardly been able to realise your presence yet. I remember a story which—'

The vicar suddenly stopped. He had forgotten it was Sunday, and would probably have gone on in his weekday mode of thought had not a turn in the breeze blown the skirt of his college gown within the range of his vision, and so reminded him. He at once diverted the current of his narrative with the dexterity the occasion demanded.

'The story of the Levite who journeyed to Beth-lehem-judah, from which I took my text the Sunday before last, is quite to the point,' he continued, with the pronunciation of a man who, far from having intended to tell a weekday story a moment earlier, had thought of nothing but Sabbath matters for several weeks. 'What did he gain after all by his restlessness? Had he remained in the city of the Jebusites, and not been so anxious for Gibeah, none of his troubles would have arisen.'

'But he had wasted five days already,' said Knight, closing his eyes to the vicar's commendable diversion. 'His fault lay in beginning the tarrying system originally.'

'True, true; my illustration fails.'

'But not the hospitality which prompted the story.'

'So you are to come just the same,' urged Mrs. Swancourt, for she had seen an almost imperceptible fall of countenance in her stepdaughter at Knight's announcement.

Knight half promised to call on his return journey; but the uncertainty with which he spoke was quite enough to fill Elfride with a regretful interest in all he did during the few remaining hours. The curate having already officiated twice that day in the two churches, Mr. Swancourt had undertaken the whole of the evening service, and Knight read the lessons for him. The sun streamed across from the dilapidated west window, and lighted all the assembled worshippers with a golden glow, Knight as he read being illuminated by the same mellow lustre. Elfride regarded him with a throbbing sadness of mood which was fed by a sense of being far removed from his sphere. As he went deliberately through the chapter appointed—a portion of the history of Elijah—and ascended that magnificent climax of the wind, the earthquake, the fire, and the still small voice, his deep tones echoed past with such apparent disregard of her existence, that his presence inspired her with a forlorn sense of unapproachableness, which his absence would hardly have been able to cause.

At the same time, turning her face for a moment to catch the glory of the dying sun as it fell on his face, her eyes were arrested by the shape and aspect of a woman in the west gallery. It was the bleak barren countenance of the widow Jethway, whom Elfride had not seen much of since the morning of her return with Stephen Smith. Possessing the smallest of competencies, this unhappy woman appeared to spend her life in journeyings between Endelstow churchyard and that of a village near Southampton, where her father and mother were laid.

She had not attended the service here for a considerable time, and she now seemed to have a reason for her choice of seat. From the gallery window the tomb of her son was plainly visible — standing as the nearest object in a prospect which was closed outwardly by the changeless horizon of the sea.

The streaming rays, too, flooded her face, now bent towards Elfride with a hard and bitter expression that the solemnity of the place raised to a tragic dignity it did not intrinsically possess. The girl resumed her normal attitude with an added disquiet.

Elfride's emotion was cumulative, and after a while would assert itself on a sudden. A slight touch was enough to set it free—a poem, a sunset, a cunningly contrived chord of music, a vague imagining, being the usual accidents of its exhibition. The longing for Knight's respect, which was leading up to an incipient yearning for his love, made the present conjuncture a sufficient one. Whilst kneeling down previous to leaving, when the sunny streaks had gone upward to the roof, and the lower part of the church was in soft shadow, she could not help thinking of Coleridge's morbid poem the 'Three Graves,' and shuddering as she wondered if Mrs. Jethway were cursing her, she wept as if her heart would break.

They came out of church just as the sun went down, leaving the landscape like a platform from which an eloquent speaker has retired, and nothing remains for the audience to do but to rise and go home. Mr. and Mrs. Swancourt went off in the carriage, Knight and Elfride preferring to walk, as the skilful old matchmaker had imagined. They descended the hill together.

'I liked your reading, Mr. Knight,' Elfride presently found herself saying. 'You read better than papa.'

'I will praise anybody that will praise me. You played excellently, Miss Swancourt, and very correctly.'

'Correctly—yes.'

'It must be a great pleasure to you to take an active part in the service.'

'I want to be able to play with more feeling. But I have not a good selection of music, sacred or secular. I wish I had a nice little music-library—well chosen, and that the only new pieces sent me were those of genuine merit.'

'I am glad to hear such a wish from you. It is extraordinary how many women have no honest love of music as an end and not as a means, even leaving out those who have nothing in them. They mostly like it for its accessories. I have never met a woman who loves music as do ten or a dozen men I know.'

'How would you draw the line between women with something and women with nothing in them?'

'Well,' said Knight, reflecting a moment, 'I mean by nothing in them those who don't care about anything solid. This is an instance: I knew a man who had a young friend he was much interested in; in fact, they were going to be married. She was seemingly poetical, and he offered her a choice of two editions of the British poets, which she pretended to want badly. He said, "Which of them would you like best for me to send?" She said, "A pair of the prettiest ear-rings in Bond-street, if you don't mind, would be nicer than either." Now I call her a girl with not much in her but vanity; and so do you, I daresay.'

'O yes,' replied Elfride with an effort.

Happening to catch a glimpse of her face as she was speaking, and noticing that her attempt at heartiness was a miserable failure, he appeared to have misgivings.

'You, Miss Swancourt, would not, under such circumstances, have preferred the nicknacks?'

'No, I don't think I should, indeed,' she stammered.

'I'll put it to you,' said the inflexible Knight. 'Which will you have of these two things of about equal value—the well-chosen little library of the best music you spoke of—bound in morocco, walnut case, lock and key—or a pair of the very prettiest ear-rings in Bond-street windows?'

'Of course the music,' Elfride replied with forced earnestness.

'You are quite certain?' he said emphatically.

'Quite,' she faltered; 'if I could for certain buy the ear-rings afterwards.'

Knight, somewhat blamably, keenly enjoyed sparring with the palpitating flexuous creature, whose excitable nature made any such thing a species of cruelty.

He looked at her rather oddly, and said, 'Fie!'

'Forgive me,' she said, laughing a little, a little frightened, and blushing very deeply.

'Ah, Miss Elfie, why didn't you say at first, as any firm woman would have said, I am as bad as she, and shall choose the same?'

'I don't know,' said Elfride wofully, and with a distressful smile.

'I thought you were exceptionally musical?'

'So I am, I think. But the test is so severe—quite painful.'

'I don't understand.'

'Music doesn't do any real good, or rather—'

'That *is* a thing to say, Miss Swancourt! Why what—'

'You don't understand! you don't understand!'

'Why, what conceivable use is there in jimcrack jewelry?'

'No, no, no, no!' she cried petulantly; 'I didn't mean what you think. I like the music best, only I like—'

'Ear-rings better—own it!' he said, in a teasing tone. 'Well, I think I should have had the moral courage to own it at once, without pretending to an elevation I could not reach.'

Like the French soldiery, Elfride was not brave when on the defensive. So it was almost with tears in her eyes that she answered desperately:

'My meaning is, that I like ear-rings best just now, because I lost one of my prettiest pair last year, and papa said he would not buy any more, or allow me to myself, because I was careless; and now

I wish I had some like them—that's what my meaning is—indeed it is, Mr. Knight.'

'I am afraid I have been very harsh and rude,' said Knight, with a look of regret at seeing how disturbed she was. 'But seriously, if women only knew how they ruin their good looks by such appurtenances, I am sure they would never want them.'

'They were lovely, and became me so!'

'Not if they were like the ordinary hideous things women stuff their ears with nowadays—like the governor of a steam-engine, or a pair of scales, or gold gibbets and chains, and artists' palettes, and compensation pendulums, and Heaven knows what besides.'

'No; they were not one of those things. So pretty—like this,' she said with eager animation. And she drew with the point of her parasol an enlarged view of one of the lamented darlings, to a scale that would have suited a giantess half-a-mile high.

'Yes, very pretty—very,' said Knight dryly. 'How did you come to lose such a precious pair of articles?'

'I only lost one—nobody ever loses both at the same time.'

She made this remark with embarrassment, and a nervous movement of the fingers. Seeing that the loss occurred whilst Stephen Smith was attempting to kiss her for the first time on the cliff, her confusion was hardly to be wondered at. The question had been awkward, and received no direct answer.

Knight seemed not to notice her manner.

'O, nobody ever loses both — I see. And certainly the fact that it was a case of loss takes away all odour of vanity from your choice.'

'As I never know whether you are in earnest, I don't now,' she said, looking up inquiringly at the hairy face of the oracle. And coming gallantly to her own rescue;

'If I really seem vain, it is that I am only vain in my ways—not in my heart. The worst women are those vain in their hearts, and not in their ways.'

'An adroit distinction. Well, they are certainly the more objectionable of the two,' said Knight.

'Is vanity a mortal or a venial sin? You know what life is: tell me.'

'I am very far from knowing what life is. A just conception of life is too large a thing to grasp during the short interval of passing through it.'

'Will the fact of a woman being fond of jewelry be likely to make her life, in its higher sense, a failure?'

'Nobody's life is altogether a failure.'

'Well, you know what I mean, even though my words are badly selected and commonplace,' she said impatiently. 'Because I utter commonplace words, you must not suppose I think only commonplace thoughts. My poor stock of words are like a limited number of rough moulds I have to cast all my materials in, good and bad; and the novelty or delicacy of the substance is often lost in the coarse triteness of the form.'

'Very well; I'll believe that ingenious representation. As to the subject in hand —lives which are failures—you need not trouble yourself. Anybody's life may be just as romantic and strange and interesting if he or she fails as if he or she succeed. All the difference is, that the last chapter is wanting in the story. If a man of power tries to do a great deed, and just falls short of it by an accident not his fault, up to that time his history had as much in it as that of a great man who has done his great deed. It is whimsical of the world to hold that particulars of how a lad went to school and so on should be as an interesting romance or as nothing to them, precisely as the lad in after years becomes renowned, or, with the power to become so, does not.'

They were walking between the sunset and the moonrise. With the dropping of the sun a nearly full moon had begun to raise itself. Their shadows, as cast by the western glare, showed signs of becoming obliterated in the interest of a rival pair in the opposite direction which the moon was bringing to distinctness.

'I consider my life to some extent a failure,' said Knight again after a pause, during which he had noticed the antagonistic shadows.

'You! How?'

'I don't precisely know. But in some way I have missed the mark.'

'Really? To have done it is not much to be sad about, but to feel that you have done it must be a cause of sorrow. Am I right?'

'Partly, though not quite. For a sensation of being profoundly experienced serves as a sort of consolation to people who are conscious of having taken wrong turnings. Contradictory as it seems, there is nothing truer than that people who have always gone right don't know half as much about the nature and ways of going right as those who have gone wrong. However, it is not desirable for me to chill your summer-time by going into this.'

'You have not told me even now if I am really vain.'

'If I say Yes, I shall offend you; if I say No, you'll think I don't mean it,' he replied, looking curiously into her face.

'Ah, well,' she replied, with a little breath of distress, '"That which is exceeding deep, who shall find it out?" I suppose I must take you as I do the Bible—find out and understand all I can; and on the strength of that swallow the rest in a lump, by simple faith. Think me vain, if you will. Worldly greatness requires so much littleness to grow up in, that an infirmity more or less is not a matter for regret.'

'As regards women, I can't say,' answered Knight carelessly; 'but it is without doubt a misfortune for a man, who has a living to get, to be born of a truly noble nature. A high soul will bring a man to the workhouse; so you may be right in sticking up for vanity.'

'No, no, I don't do that,' she said regretfully. 'Mr. Knight, when you are gone, will you send me something you have written? I think I should like to see whether you write as you have lately spoken, or in your better mood. Which is your true self —the cynic you have been this evening, or the nice philosopher you were up to tonight?'

'Ah, which? You know as well as I.'

Their conversation detained them on the lawn and in the portico till the stars blinked out. Elfride flung back her head, and said idly,

'There's a bright star exactly over me.'

'Each bright star is overhead somewhere.'

'Is it? O yes, of course. Where is that one?' and she pointed with her finger.

'That is poised like a white hawk over one of the Cape Verde islands.'

'And that?'

'Looking down upon the source of the Nile.

'And that lonely quiet-looking one?'

'He watches the North Pole, and has no less than the whole equator for his horizon. And that idle one low down upon the ground, that we have almost rolled away from, is in India—over the head of a young friend of mine, who very possibly looks at the star in our zenith, as it hangs low upon his horizon, and thinks of it as marking where his true-love dwells.'

Elfride glanced at Knight with misgiving. Did he mean her? She could not see his features; but his attitude seemed to show unconsciousness.

'The star is over *my* head,' she said with hesitation.

'Or anybody else's in England.'

'O yes, I see,' with a breath of relief.

'His parents, I believe, are natives of this county. I don't know them, though I have been in correspondence with him for many years till lately. Fortunately or unfortunately for him he fell in love, and then went to Bombay. Since that time I have heard very little of him.'

Knight went no farther in his volunteered statement, and though Elfride at one moment was inclined to profit by the lessons in honesty he had just been giving her, the flesh was weak, and the intention dispersed into silence. There seemed a reproach in Knight's blind words, and yet she was not able to clearly define any disloyalty she had been guilty of.

CHAPTER VII.

'A DISTANT DEARNESS IN THE HILL.'

KNIGHT turned his back upon the parish of Endelstow, and crossed over to Cork.

One day of absence superimposed itself on another, and proportionately weighted his heart. He pushed on to the Lakes of Killarney, rambled amid their luxuriant woods, surveyed the infinite variety of island, hill, and dale to be there found, listened to the marvellous echoes of that romantic spot; but altogether missed the glory and the dream he formerly found in such favoured regions.

Whilst in the company of Elfride, her girlish presence had not perceptibly affected him to any depth. He had not been conscious that her entry into his sphere had added anything to himself; but now that she was taken away he was very conscious of a great deal being abstracted. The superfluity had become a necessity, and Knight was in love.

Stephen fell in love with Elfride by looking at her: Knight by ceasing to do so. When or how the spirit entered into him he knew not: certain he was that when on the point of leaving Endelstow he had felt none of that exquisite nicety of poignant sadness natural to such severances, seeing how delightful a subject of contemplation Elfride had been ever since. Had he begun to love her when she met his eye after her mishap on the tower? He had simply thought her weak. Had he grown to love her whilst standing on the lawn brightened all over by the evening sun? He had thought her complexion good: no more. Was it her conversation that had sown the seed? He had thought her words ingenious, and very creditable to a young woman, but not noteworthy. Had the chess-playing anything to do with it? Certainly not: he had thought her at that time a rather conceited child.

Knight's experience was a complete disproof of the assumption that love always comes by glances of the eye and sympathetic touches of the fingers: that, like flame, it makes itself palpable at the moment of generation. Not till they were parted, and she had become sublimated in his memory, could he be said to have even attentively regarded her.

Thus, having passively gathered up images of her which his mind did not act upon till the cause of them was no longer before him, he appeared to himself to have fallen in love with her soul, which had temporarily assumed its disembodiment to accompany him on his way.

She began to rule him so imperiously now that, accustomed to analysis, he almost trembled at the possible result of the introduction of this new force among the nicely adjusted ones of his ordinary life. He became restless: then he forgot all collateral subjects in the pleasure of thinking about her.

Yet it must be said that Knight loved philosophically rather than with romance.

He thought of her manner towards him. Simplicity verges on coquetry. Was she flirting? he said to himself. No forcible translation of favour into suspicion was able to uphold such a theory. The performance had been too well done to be anything but real. It had the defects without which nothing is genuine. No actress of twenty years' standing, no bald-necked lady whose earliest season 'out' was lost in the discreet mist of evasive talk, could have played before him the part of ingenuous girl as Elfride lived it. She had the little artful ways which partly make up ingenuousness.

There are bachelors by nature and bachelors by circumstance: spinsters there doubtless are also of both kinds, though I have only met those of the latter. However, Knight had been looked upon as a bachelor by nature. What was he coming to? It was very odd to himself to look at his theories on the subject of love, and reading them now by the full light of a new experience, to see how much more his sentences meant than he had felt them to mean when they were written. People often discover the real force of a trite old maxim only when it is thrust upon them by a chance adventure; but Knight had never before known the case of a man who learnt the full compass of his own epigrams by such means.

He was intensely satisfied with one aspect of the affair. Inbred in him was an invincible objection to be any but the first comer in a woman's heart. He had discovered within himself the condition that if ever he did make up his mind to marry, it must be on the certainty that no cropping out of inconvenient old letters, no bow and blush to a mysterious stranger casually met, should be a possible source of discomposure. Knight's sentiments were only the ordinary ones of a man of his age who loves genuinely, perhaps exaggerated a little by his pursuits. When men first love as lads, it is with the very centre of their hearts, nothing else being concerned in the operation. With added years, more of the faculties attempt a partnership in the passion, till at Knight's age the understanding is fain to have a hand in it. It may as well be left out. A man in love setting up his brains as a gauge of his position is as one determining a ship's longitude from a light at the mast-head.

Knight argued from Elfride's unwontedness of manner, which was matter of fact, to an unwontedness in love, which was matter of inference only. *Incrédules les plus crédules.* 'Elfride,' he said, 'had hardly looked upon a man till she saw me.'

He had never forgotten his severity to her because she preferred ornament to edification, and had since excused her a hundred times by thinking how natural to womankind was a love of adornment, and how necessary became a mild infusion of personal vanity to complete the delicate and fascinating dye of the feminine mind. So at the end of the week's absence, which had brought him as far as Dublin, he resolved to curtail his tour, return to Endelstow, and commit himself by making a reality of the hypothetical offer of that Sunday evening.

Notwithstanding that he had concocted a great deal of paper theory on social amenities and modern manners generally, the special ounce of practice was wanting, and now for his life Knight could not recollect whether it was considered correct to give a young lady personal ornaments before a regular engagement to marry had been initiated. But the day before leaving Dublin he looked around anxiously for a high-class jewelry establishment, in which he purchased what he considered would suit her best.

It was with a most awkward and unwonted feeling that after entering and closing the door of his room he sat down, opened the morocco case, and held up each of the fragile bits of gold-work before his eyes. Many things had become old to the solitary man of letters, but these were new, and he handled like a child an outcome of civilisation which had never before been touched by his fingers. A sudden fastidious decision that the pattern chosen would not suit her after all caused him to rise in a flurry and tear down the street to change them for others. After a great deal of trouble in re-selecting, during which his mind became so bewildered that the critical faculty on objects of art seemed to have vacated his person altogether, Knight carried off another pair of ear-rings. These remained in his possession till the afternoon, when, after contemplating them fifty times with a growing misgiving that the last choice was worse than the first, he felt that no sleep would visit his pillow till he had improved upon his previous purchases yet again. In a perfect heat of vexation with himself for such tergiversation, he went anew to the shop-door, was absolutely ashamed to enter and give further trouble, went to another shop, bought a pair at an enormously increased price because they seemed the very thing, asked the goldsmiths if they would take the other pair in exchange, was told that they could not exchange articles bought of another maker, paid down the money, and went off with the two pairs in his possession, wondering what on earth to do with the superfluous pair. He almost wished he could lose them, or that somebody would steal them, and was burdened with an interposing sense that, as a capable man, with true ideas of economy, he must necessarily sell them somewhere. Mingled with a blank feeling of a whole day being lost to him in running about the city on this new and extraordinary class of errand, and of several pounds being lost through his bungling, was a slight sense of satisfaction that he had emerged for ever from his antediluvian ignorance on the subject of ladies' jewelry, as well as secured a truly artistic production at last. During the remainder of that day he scanned the ornaments of every lady he met with the profoundly experienced eye of an appraiser.

Next morning Knight was again crossing St. George's Channel—not returning to London by the Holyhead route as he had originally intended, but towards Bristol—availing himself of Mr. and Mrs. Swancourt's invitation to revisit them on his homeward journey.

We flit forward to Elfride.

Woman's ruling passion—to fascinate and influence those more powerful than she—though operant in Elfride, was decidedly purposeless. She had wanted her friend Knight's good opinion from the first: how much more than that elementary ingredient of friendship she now desired, her fears would hardly allow her to think. In originally wishing to please the highest class of man she had ever intimately known, there was no disloyalty to Stephen Smith. She could not — and few women can — realise the possible vastness of an issue which has only an insignificant begetting.

Her letters from Stephen were necessarily few, and her sense of fidelity clung to the last she had received as a wrecked mariner clings to flotsam. The young girl persuaded herself that she was glad Stephen had such a right to her hand as he had acquired (in her eyes) by the elopement. She beguiled herself by saying, 'Perhaps if I had not so committed myself I might fall in love with Mr. Knight.'

All this made the week of Knight's absence very gloomy and distasteful to her. She retained Stephen in her prayers, and his old letters were re-read—as a medicine in reality, though she deceived herself into the belief that it was as a pleasure.

These letters had grown more and more hopeful. He told her that he finished work every day with a pleasant consciousness of having removed one more stone from the barrier which divided them. Then he drew images of what a fine figure they two would cut some day. People would turn their heads and say, 'What a prize he has won!' She was not to be sad about that wild runaway attempt of theirs (Elfride had repeatedly said that it grieved her). Whatever any other person who knew of it might think, he knew well enough the modesty of her nature. The only reproach was a gentle one for not having written quite so devotedly during her visit to London. Her letter had seemed to have a liveliness derived from other thoughts than thoughts of him.

Knight's intention of an early return to Endelstow having originally been faint, his promise to do so had been fainter.

He was a man who kept his words well to the rear of his possible actions. The vicar was rather surprised to see him again so soon: Mrs. Swancourt was not. Knight found, on meeting them all, after his arrival had been announced, that they had formed an intention to go to St. Leonards for a few days at the end of the month.

No satisfactory conjuncture offered itself on this first evening of his return for presenting Elfride with what he had been at such pains to procure. He was fastidious in his reading of opportunities for such a nearing act. The next morning chancing to break fine after a week of cloudy weather, it was proposed and decided that they should all drive to Barwith Bay, a local lion which neither Mrs. Swancourt nor Knight had seen. Knight scented romantic occasions from afar, and foresaw that such a one might be expected before the coming night.

The journey was along a road by neutral green hills, upon which hedgerows lay trailing like ropes on a quay. Gaps in these uplands revealed the blue sea, flecked with a few dashes of white and a solitary white sail, the whole brimming up to a keen horizon which lay like a line ruled from hill-side to hill-side. Then they rolled down a pass, the chocolate-toned rocks forming a wall on both sides, from one of which fell a heavy jagged shade over half the roadway. A spout of fresh water burst from an occasional crevice, and pattering down upon broad green leaves, ran along as a rivulet at the bottom. Unkempt locks of heather overhung the brow of each steep, whence at divers points a bramble swung forth into mid-air, snatching at their head-dresses like a claw.

They mounted the last crest, and the bay which was to be the end of their pilgrimage burst upon them. The ocean blueness deepened its colour as it stretched to the feet of the crags, where it terminated in a fringe of white—silent at this distance, though moving and heaving like a counterpane upon a restless sleeper. The shadowed hollows of the purple-and-brown rocks would have been called blue had not that tint been so entirely appropriated by the water beside them.

The carriage was put up at a little cottage with a shed attached, and an ostler and the coachman carried the hamper of provisions down to the shore.

Knight found his opportunity. 'I did not forget your wish,' he began, when they were apart from their friends.

Elfride looked as if she did not understand.

'And I have brought you these,' he continued, awkwardly pulling out the case, and opening it while holding it towards her.

'O Mr. Knight,' said Elfride, confused, and turning to a lively red; 'I didn't know you had any intention or meaning in what you said. I thought it a mere supposition. I don't want them.'

A thought which had flashed into her mind gave the reply a greater decisiveness than it might otherwise have possessed. To-morrow was the day for Stephen's letter.

'But will you not accept them?' Knight returned, feeling less her master than heretofore.

'I would rather not. They are beautiful—more beautiful than any I have ever seen,' she answered earnestly, looking half-wishfully at the temptation, as Eve may have looked at the apple. 'But I don't want to have them, if you will kindly forgive me, Mr. Knight.'

'No kindness at all,' said Mr. Knight, brought to a full-stop at this unexpected turn of events.

A silence followed. Knight held the open case, looking rather wofully at the glittering forms he had forsaken his orbit to procure; turning it about and holding it up as if, feeling his gift to be slighted by her, he were endeavouring to admire it very much himself.

'Shut them up, and don't let me see them any longer—do!' she said laughingly, and with a quaint mixture of reluctance and entreaty.

'Why, Elfie?'

'Not Elfie to you, Mr. Knight. O, because I shall want them. There, I am silly, I know, to say that. But I have a reason for not taking them—now.' She kept in the last word for a moment, intending to imply that her refusal was finite, but somehow the word slipped out, and undid all the rest.

'You will take them some day?'

'I don't want to.'

'Why don't you want to, Elfride Swancourt?'

'Because I don't. I don't like to take them.'

'I have read a fact of distressing significance in that,' said Knight. 'Since you like them, your dislike to having them must be towards me?'

'No, it isn't.'

'What, then, do you like me?'

Elfride deepened her tint and looked into the distance with features shaped to an expression of the nicest criticism as regarded her answer.

'I like you pretty well,' she at length murmured mildly.

'Not very much?'

'You are so sharp with me, and say hard things, and so how can I?' she replied evasively.

'You think me a fogey, I suppose?'

'No, I don't—I mean I do—I don't know what I think you, I mean. Let us go to papa,' responded Elfride, with somewhat of a flurried delivery.

'Well, I'll tell you my object in getting the present,' said Knight, with a composure intended to remove from her mind any possible impression of his being what he was—her lover. 'You see it was the very least I could do in common civility.'

Elfride felt rather blank at this lucid statement.

Knight continued, putting away the case, 'I felt as anybody naturally would have, you know, that my words on your choice the other day were invidious and unfair, and thought an apology should take a practical shape.'

'O yes.'

Elfride was sorry—she could not tell why—that he gave such a legitimate reason. It was a disappointment that he had all the time a cool motive, which might be stated to anybody without raising a smile. Had she known they were offered in that spirit, she would certainly have accepted the seductive gift. And the tantalising feature was that perhaps he suspected her to imagine them offered as a lover's token, which was mortifying enough if they were not.

Mrs. Swancourt came now to where they were sitting, to select a point for spreading their table, and, amid the discussion upon that subject, the matter pending between Knight and Elfride was shelved for a while. He read her refusal so certainly as the bashfulness of a girl in a novel position, that upon the whole he could tolerate such a beginning. Could Knight have been told that it was a sense of fidelity struggling against new love, whilst no less assuring as to his ultimate victory, it would have entirely abstracted the wish to secure it.

At the same time a slight constraint of manner was visible in them for the remainder of the afternoon. The tide turned, and they were obliged to ascend to higher ground. The day glided on to its end in the usual quiet dreamy passivity of such occasions—when every deed done and thing thought is in endeavouring to avoid doing and thinking more. Looking idly over the verge of a crag, they beheld their diningtable gradually being splashed upon and their crumbs and fragments all washed away by the incoming sea. The vicar drew a moral lesson from the scene; Knight replied in the same satisfied strain. And then the waves rolled in furiously—the neutral green-and-blue tongues of water slid up the slopes, and were metamorphosed into foam by a careless blow, falling back white and faint, and leaving trailing followers behind.

The passing of a heavy shower was the next scene—driving them to shelter in a shallow cave—after which the horses were put in, and they started to return homeward. By the time they reached the higher levels, the sky had again cleared, and the sunset rays glanced directly upon the wet uphill road they had climbed. The ruts formed by their carriage-wheels on the ascent—a pair of Liliputian canals—were as so many shining bars of gold, tapering to nothing in the distance. Upon this also they turned their backs, and night spread over the sea.

The evening was chilly, and there was no moon. Knight sat close to Elfride, and, when the darkness rendered the position of a person a matter of uncertainty, particularly close. Elfride edged away.

'I hope you allow me my place ungrudgingly?' he whispered.

'O yes; 'tis the least I can do in common civility,' she said, accenting the words so that he might recognise them as his own returned.

Both of them felt delicately balanced between two possibilities. Thus they reached home.

To Knight this mild experience was delightful. It was to him a gentle innocent time—a time which, though there may not be much in it, seldom repeats itself in a man's life, and has a peculiar dearness when glanced at retrospectively. He is not inconveniently deep in love, and is lulled by a peaceful sense of being able to enjoy the most trivial thing with a childlike enjoyment. The movement of a wave, the colour of a stone, anything, was enough for Knight's drowsy thoughts of that day to precipitate themselves upon. Even the sermonising platitudes the vicar had delivered himself of—chiefly because something seemed to be professionally required of him in the presence of a man of Knight's proclivities—were swallowed whole. The presence of Elfride led him not merely to tolerate that kind of talk from the necessities of ordinary courtesy; but he listened to it—took in the ideas with an enjoyable make-believe that they were proper and necessary, and indulged in a conservative feeling that the face of things was complete

Entering her room that evening, Elfride found a packet for herself on the dressing-table. How it came there she did not know. She tremblingly undid the folds of white paper that covered it. Yes; it was the treasure of a morocco case, containing those treasures of ornament she had refused in the daytime.

Elfride dressed herself in them for a moment, looked at herself in the glass, blushed red, and put them away. They filled her dreams all that night. Never had she seen anything so lovely, and never was it more clear that as an honest woman she was in duty bound to refuse them. Why it was not equally clear to her that duty required more vigorous coördinate conduct as well, let those who dissect her say.

The next morning glared in like a spectre upon her. It was Stephen's letter-day, and she was bound to meet the postman—to stealthily do a deed she had never liked, to secure an end she now had ceased to desire.

But she went.

There were two letters.

One was from the bank at St. Kirrs, in

which she had a small private deposit—probably something about interest. She put that in her pocket for a moment, and going indoors and up-stairs, to be safer from observation, tremblingly opened Stephen's.

What was this he said to her?

She was to go to the St. Kirrs Bank and take a sum of money which they had received private advices to pay her.

The sum was two hundred pounds.

There was no cheque, order, or anything of the nature of guarantee. In fact the information amounted to this: the money was now in the St. Kirrs Bank, standing in her name.

She instantly opened the other letter. It contained a deposit-note from the bank for the sum of two hundred pounds which had that day been added to her account. Stephen's information, then, was correct, and the transfer made.

'I have earned this in one year,' Stephen's letter went on to say, 'and what so proper as well as pleasant for me to do as to hand it over to you to keep for your use? I have plenty for myself, independently of this. Should you not be disposed to let it lie idle in the bank, get your father to invest it in your name on good security. It is a little present to you from your more than betrothed. He will, I think, Elfride, feel now that my pretensions to your hand are anything but the dream of a silly boy, not worth rational consideration.'

With a natural delicacy, Elfride, in mentioning her father's marriage, had refrained from all allusion to the pecuniary resources of the lady.

Leaving this matter-of-fact subject, he went on, somewhat after his boyish manner:

'Do you remember, darling, that first morning of my arrival at your house, when your father read at prayers the miracle of healing the sick of the palsy—where he is told to take up his bed and walk? I do, and I can now so well realise the force of that passage. The smallest piece of mat is the bed of the Oriental, and yesterday I saw a native perform the very action, which reminded me to mention it. But you are better read than I, and perhaps you knew all this long ago. . . . . One day I bought some small native idols to send home to you as curiosities, but afterwards finding they had been cast in England, made to look old, and shipped over, I threw them away in disgust.

'Speaking of this reminds me that we are obliged to import all our house-building ironwork from England. Never was such foresight required to be exercised in building houses as here. Before we begin, we have to order every column, lock, hinge, and screw that will be required. We cannot go into the next street, as in London, and get them cast at a minute's notice. Mr. L. says somebody will have to go to England very soon and superintend the selection of a large order of this kind. I only wish I may be the man.'

There before her lay the deposit-receipt for the two hundred pounds, and beside it the elegant present of Knight. Elfride grew cold—then her cheeks felt heated by beating blood. If by destroying the piece of paper the whole transaction could have been withdrawn from her experience, she would willingly have sacrificed the money it represented. She did not know what to do in either case. She almost feared to let the two articles lie in juxtaposition: so antagonistic were the interests they represented that a miraculous repulsion of one by the other was almost to be expected.

That day she was seen little of. By the evening she had come to a resolution, and acted upon it. The packet was sealed up—with a tear of regret as she closed the case upon the pretty forms it contained — directed, and placed upon the writing-table in Knight's room. And a letter was written to Stephen, stating that as yet she hardly understood her position with regard to the money sent; but declaring that she was ready to fulfil her promise to marry him. After this letter had been written she delayed posting it — although never ceasing to feel strenuously that the deed must be done.

Several days passed. There was another Indian letter for Elfride. Coming unexpectedly, her father saw it, but made no remark — why, she could not tell. The news this time was absolutely overwhelming. Stephen, as he had wished, had been actually chosen as the most fitting to execute the ironwork commission he had alluded to as impending. This duty completed, he had three months' leave. His letter continued that he should follow it in a week, and should take the opportunity to plainly ask her father to permit the engagement. Then came a page expressive of his delight and hers at the reunion, and finally, the information that he would write to the shipping agents, asking them to telegraph and tell her when the ship bringing him home should be in sight — knowing how acceptable such information would be.

Elfride lived and moved now as in a dream. Knight had at first become almost angry at her persistent refusal of his offering — and no less with the manner than the fact of it. But he saw that she began to look worn and ill — and his vexation lessened to simple perplexity.

He ceased now to remain in the house for long hours together as before, but made it a mere centre for antiquarian and geological excursions in the neighbourhood. Throw up his cards and go away he fain would have done, but could not. And thus, availing himself of the privileges of a relative, he went in and out the premises as fancy led him — but still lingered on.

'I don't wish to stay here another day

if my presence is distasteful,' he said one afternoon. 'At first you used to imply that I was severe with you; and when I am kind you treat me unfairly.'

'No, no. Don't say so.'

The origin of their acquaintanceship had been such as to render their manner towards each other peculiar and uncommon. It was of a kind to cause them to speak out their minds on any feelings of objection and difference: to be reticent on gentler matters.

'I have a good mind to go away and never trouble you again,' continued Knight.

She said nothing, but the eloquent expression of her eyes and wan face was enough to reproach him for harshness.

'Do you like me to be here, then?' inquired Knight gently.

'Yes,' she said. Fidelity to the old love and truth to the new were ranged on opposite sides, and truth virtuelessly prevailed.

'Then I'll stay a little longer,' said Knight.

'Don't be vexed if I keep by myself a good deal, will you? Perhaps something may happen, and I may tell you something.'

'Mere coyness,' said Knight to himself; and went away with a lighter heart. The trick of reading truly the enigmatical forces at work in women at given times, which with some men is an unerring instinct, is peculiar to minds less direct and honest than Knight's.

The next evening, about five o'clock, before Knight had returned from a pilgrimage along the shore, a man walked up to the house. He was a messenger from the station at Stranton, to which place the railway had been advanced during the summer.

A telegram for Miss Swancourt, and a shilling to pay for the special messenger.

Miss Swancourt sent out the money,

signed the paper, and opened her letter with a trembling hand. She read:

'*Johnson, Liverpool, to Miss Swancourt, Endelstow, near Stranton.*

'*Amaryllis telegraphed off Holyhead, four o'clock. Expect will dock and land passengers at Canning's Basin ten o'clock to-morrow morning.*'

Her father called her into the study.

'Elfride, who sent you that message?' he asked suspiciously.

'Johnson.'

'Who is Johnson, for Heaven's sake?'

'I don't know.'

'The deuce you don't! Who is to know, then?'

'I have never heard of him till now.'

'That's a singular story, isn't it?'

'I don't know.'

'Come, come, miss! What was the telegram?'

'Do you really wish to know, papa?'

'Well, I do.'

'Remember, I am a full-grown woman now.'

'Well, what then?'

'Being a woman, and not a child, I may, I think, have a secret or two.'

'You will, it seems.'

'Women have, as a rule.'

'But don't keep them. So speak out.'

'If you will not press me now, I give my word to tell you the meaning of all this before the week is past.'

'On your honour?'

'On my honour.'

'Very well. I have had a certain suspicion, you know; and I shall be glad to find it false. I don't like your manner lately.'

'At the end of the week, I said, papa.'

Her father did not reply, and Elfride left the room.

She began to look out for the postman again. The next morning but one he brought an inland letter from Stephen. It contained very little matter, having been written in haste; but the meaning was bulky enough. Stephen said he should arrive at his father's house, East Endelstow, at five or six o'clock that same evening; that he would after dusk walk on to the next village, and meet her, if she would, in the church porch, as in the old time. He proposed this plan because he thought it unadvisable to call formally at her house so late in the evening; yet he could not sleep without having seen her. The minutes would seem hours till he clasped her in his arms.

Elfride was still steadfast in her opinion that honour compelled her to meet him. Probably the very longing to avoid him lent additional weight to the conviction; for she was markedly one of those who sigh for the unattainable—to whom, superlatively, a hope is pleasing because not a possession. And she knew it so well, that her intellect was inclined to exaggerate this defect in herself.

So during the day she looked her duty steadfastly in the face; read Wordsworth's astringent yet depressing ode to that Deity; committed herself to her guidance; and still felt the weight of chance desires.

But she began to take a melancholy pleasure in contemplating the sacrifice of herself to the man whom a maidenly sense of propriety compelled her to regard as her only possible husband. She would meet him, and do all that lay in her power to marry him. To guard against a relapse, a note was at once despatched to his father's cottage for Stephen on his arrival, naming an hour for the interview.

CHAPTER VIII.

'ON THY COLD GRAY STONES, O SEA!'

STEPHEN had said that he should come by way of Bristol, and thence by the steamer to Stranton, in order to avoid the long journey over the hills from St. Kirrs. He did not know of the extension of the railway.

During the afternoon a thought occurred to Elfride, that from any cliff along the shore it would be possible to see the steamer some hours before its arrival.

She had accumulated religious force enough to do an act of supererogation. The act was this—to go to some point of land and watch for the ship that brought her future husband home.

It was a cloudy afternoon. Elfride was

often diverted from a purpose by a dull sky; and though she used to persuade herself that the weather was as fine as possible on the other side of the clouds, she could not bring about any practical result from this fancy. Now her mood was such that the humid sky harmonised.

Having ascended and passed over a hill behind the house, Elfride came to a small stream. She used it as a guide to the coast. It was smaller than that in her own valley, and flowed altogether at a higher level. Furze-bushes lined the slopes of its shallow trough; but at the bottom, where the water flowed, was a soft green carpet, in a strip two or three yards wide.

In winter, the water flowed over the grass; in summer, as now, it trickled along a channel in the midst.

Elfride had a sensation of eyes regarding her from somewhere. She turned, and there was Mr. Knight. He had dropped into the valley from the side of the hill.

She felt a thrill of pleasure, and rebelliously allowed it to exist.

'What utter loneliness to find you in!'

'I am going to the shore by tracking the stream. I believe it empties itself not far off, in a silver thread of water, over a cascade of great height.'

'Why do you load yourself with that heavy telescope?'

'To look over the sea with it,' she said faintly.

'I'll carry it for you to your journey's end.' And he took the glass from her unresisting hands. 'It cannot be half a mile farther. See, there is the water.' He pointed to a short fragment of level muddy-gray colour, cutting against the sky.

Elfride had already scanned the small surface of ocean visible, and had seen no ship.

They walked along in company, sometimes with the brook between them—for it was no wider than a man's stride—sometimes close together. The green carpet grew swampy, and they kept higher up.

One of the two ridges between which they walked dwindled lower and became insignificant. That on the right hand rose with their advance, and terminated in a clearly-defined edge against the light, as if it were abruptly sawn off. A little farther, and the bed of the rivulet ended in the same fashion.

They had come to a bank breast-high, and over it the valley was no longer to be seen. It was withdrawn, cleanly and completely. In its place was sky and boundless atmosphere; and perpendicularly down beneath them—small and far off—lay the corrugated surface of the Atlantic.

The small stream here found its death. Running over the precipice it was dispersed in spray before it was half way down, and falling like rain upon projecting ledges, made minute grassy meadows of them.

Lower down it soaked away amid the débris of the cliff. This was the inglorious end of the river.

'What are you looking for?' said Knight, following the direction of her eyes.

She was gazing hard at a black object—nearer to the shore than to the horizon—from the summit of which came a nebulous haze, stretching like gauze over the sea.

'The *Puffin* steamboat—from Bristol to Stranton,' she said. 'I think that is it—look. Will you give me the glass?'

Knight pulled open the old-fashioned but powerful telescope, and handed it to Elfride, who had looked on with heavy eyes.

'I can't keep it up, now,' she said.

'Rest it on my shoulder.'

'It is too high.'

'Under my arm.'

'Too low. You may look instead,' she murmured weakly.

Knight raised the glass to his eye, and

swept the sea till the *Puffin* entered its field.

'Yes, it is the *Puffin*. I can see her figure-head distinctly—a bird with a beak as big as its head.'

'Can you see the deck?'

'Wait a minute; yes, pretty clearly. And I can see the black forms of the passengers against its white surface. One of them has taken something from another—a glass, I think—yes, it is—and he is levelling it in this direction. Depend upon it we are conspicuous objects against the sky to them. Now it seems to rain upon them, and they put on overcoats and open umbrellas. They vanish and go below—all but that one who has borrowed the glass. He is a slim young fellow, and still watches us.'

Elfride grew pale, and shifted her little feet uneasily.

Knight lowered the glass.

'I think we had better return,' he said.

'That cloud which is raining on them may soon reach us. Why, you look ill. How is that?'

'Something in the air affects my face.'

'Those fair cheeks are very fastidious, I fear,' returned Knight tenderly. 'This air would make those rosy that were never so before, one would think—eh, Nature's spoilt child?'

Elfride's colour returned again.

'There is more to see behind us, after all,' said Knight.

She turned her back upon the boat and Stephen Smith, and saw, towering still higher than themselves, the vertical face of the hill on the right, which did not project seaward so far as the bed of the valley, but formed the back of a small cove, and so was visible like a concave wall, bending round from their position towards the left.

The composition of the huge hill was revealed to its backbone and marrow here at its rent extremity. It consisted of a vast stratification of blackish-gray slate, unvaried in its whole height by a single change of shade.

It is with cliffs and mountains as with persons; they have what is called a presence, which is not proportionate to their actual bulk. A little cliff will impress you powerfully: a great one not at all. It depends, as with man, upon the countenance of the cliff.

'I cannot bear to look at that cliff,' said Elfride. 'It has a horrid personality, and makes me shudder. We will go.'

'Can you climb?' said Knight. 'If so, we will ascend by that path over the grim old fellow's brow.'

'Try me,' said Elfride disdainfully. 'I have ascended steeper slopes than that.'

From where they had been loitering, a grassy path wound along inside a bank, placed as a safeguard for unwary pedestrians, to the top of the precipice, and over it along the hill in an inland direction.

'Take my arm, Miss Swancourt,' said Knight.

'I can get on better without it, thank you.'

When they were one quarter of the way up, Elfride stopped to take breath. Knight stretched out his hand.

She took it, and they ascended the remaining slope together. Reaching the very top they sat down to rest by mutual consent.

'Heavens, what an altitude!' said Knight, between his pants, and looking far over the sea. The cascade at the bottom of the slope appeared a mere span in height from where they were now.

Elfride was looking to the left. The steamboat was in full view again now, and by reason of the vast surface of sea their higher position uncovered, it seemed almost close to the shore.

'Over that edge,' said Knight, 'where nothing but vacancy appears, is a moving compact mass. The wind strikes the face of the rock, runs up it, rises like a fountain to far above our heads, curls over us in an arch, and disperses behind us. In fact, an inverted cascade is there—as perfect as the Niagara Falls—but rising instead of falling, and air instead of water. Now look here.'

Knight threw a stone over the bank, aiming it as if to go onward over the cliff. Reaching the verge, it towered into the air like a bird, turned back, and alighted on the ground behind them. They themselves were in a dead calm.

'A boat crosses Niagara immediately at the foot of the falls, where the water is quite still, the fallen mass curving under it. We are in precisely the same position with regard to our atmospheric cataract here. If you run back from the cliff fifty yards, you will be in a brisk wind. Now I daresay over the bank is a little backward current.'

Knight arose and leant over the bank.

No sooner was his head above it than his hat appeared to be sucked from his head—slipping over his forehead in a seaward direction.

'That's the backward eddy, as I told you,' he cried, and vanished over the little bank after his hat.

Elfride waited one minute; he did not return. She waited another, and there was no sign of him.

A few drops of rain fell, then a sudden shower.

She arose, and looked over the bank. On the other side were two or three yards of level ground—then a short steep preparatory slope — then the verge of the precipice.

On the slope was Knight, his hat on his head. He was on his hands and knees, trying to climb back to the level ground. The rain had wetted the shaly surface of the incline. A slight superficial wetting of soil of any kind makes it far more slippery to stand on than the same soil thoroughly drenched. The inner substance is still hard, and is lubricated by the moistened film.

'I find a difficulty in getting back,' said Knight.

Elfride's heart fell like lead.

'But you can get back?' she wildly inquired.

Knight strove with all his might for two or three minutes, and the drops of perspiration began to bead his brow.

'No, I am unable to do it,' he answered.

Elfride, by a wrench of thought, forced away from her mind the sensation that Knight was in bodily danger. But attempt to help him she must. She ventured upon the treacherous incline, propped herself with the closed telescope, and gave him her hand before he saw her movements.

'O Elfride, why did you!' said he. 'I am afraid you have only endangered yourself.'

And as if to prove his statement, in

making an endeavour by her assistance they both slipped lower, and then he was again stayed. His foot was propped by a bracket of quartz rock, balanced on the verge of the precipice. Fixed by this, he steadied her, her head being about a foot below the beginning of the slope. Elfride had dropped the glass; it rolled to the edge and vanished over it into a nether sky.

'Hold tightly to me,' he said.

She flung her arms round his neck with such a firm grasp that whilst he remained it was impossible for her to fall.

'Don't be flurried,' Knight continued. 'So long as we stay above this block we are perfectly safe. Wait a moment whilst I consider what we had better do.'

He turned his eyes to the dizzy depths beneath them, and surveyed the position of affairs.

Two glances told him a tale with ghastly distinctness. It was that, unless they performed their feat of getting up the slope with the precision of machines, they were over the edge and whirling in mid-air.

For this purpose it was necessary that he should recover the breath and strength which his previous efforts had cost him. So he still waited, and looked in the face of the enemy.

The crest of this terrible natural façade passed among the neighbouring inhabitants as being seven hundred feet above the water it overhung. It had been proved by actual measurement to be not a foot less than six hundred and fifty.

That is to say, it is nearly three times the height of Flamborough, half as high again as the South Foreland, a hundred feet higher than Beachy Head—the loftiest promontory on the east or south side of this island, twice the height of St. Alban's, thrice as high as the Lizard, and just double the height of St. Bee's. One seaboard point on the western coast is known to surpass it in altitude, but only by a few feet. This is Great Orme's Head, in Caernarvonshire.

And it must be remembered that the cliff exhibits an intensifying feature which some of those are without—sheer perpendicularity from the half-tide level.

Yet this remarkable rampart forms no headland: it rather walls in an inlet—the promontory on each side being much lower. Thus, far from being salient, its horizontal section is concave. The sea, rolling direct from the shores of North America, has in fact eaten a chasm into the middle of a hill, and the giant, embayed and unobtrusive, stands in the rear of pigmy supporters. Not least singularly, neither hill, chasm, nor precipice has a name, or the merest tradition of a name. On this account I will call the precipice the Cliff without a Name.

What gave an added terror to its height was its blackness. And upon this dark face the beating of ten thousand west winds had formed a kind of bloom, which had a visual effect not unlike that of a black Hambro' grape. Moreover it seemed to float off into the atmosphere, and inspire terror through the lungs.

'This piece of quartz, supporting my feet, is on the very nose of the cliff,' said Knight, breaking the silence after his rigid stoical meditation. 'Now what you are to do is this. Clamber up my body till your feet are on my shoulders: when you are there you will, I think, be able to climb on to level ground.'

'What will you do?'

'Wait whilst you run for assistance.'

'I ought to have done that in the first place, ought I not?'

'I was in the act of slipping, and should have reached no stand-point without your weight, in all probability. But don't let us talk. Be brave, Elfride, and climb.'

She prepared to ascend, saying, 'This

is the moment I anticipated when on the tower. I thought it would come.'

'This is not a time for superstition,' said Knight. 'Dismiss all that.'

'I will,' she said humbly.

'Now put your foot into my hand: next the other. That's good—well done. Hold to my shoulder.'

She placed her feet upon the stirrup he made of his hand, and was high enough to get a view of the natural surface of the hill over the bank.

'Can you now climb on to level ground?'

'I am afraid not. I will try.'

'What can you see?'

'The sloping common.'

'What upon it?'

'Purple heather and some grass.'

'Nothing more—no man or human being of any kind?'

'Nobody.'

'Now try to get higher in this way.

You see that tuft of sea-pink above you. Get that well into your hand, but don't trust to it entirely. Then step upon my shoulder, and I think you will reach the top.'

With trembling knees she did exactly as he told her. The preternatural quiet and solemnity of his manner overspread upon herself, and gave her a courage not her own. She made a spring from the top of his shoulder, and was up.

Then she turned to look at him.

By an ill-fate, the force downwards of her bound, added to his own weight, had been too much for the block of quartz upon which his feet depended. It was, indeed, an igneous protrusion into the enormous masses of black strata, which had been denuded from the sides of the alien fragment by centuries of frost and rain, and now left it without much support.

It moved. Knight seized a tuft of sea-pink with each hand.

The quartz rock which had been his

salvation was worse than useless now. It rolled over, out of sight, and away into the same nether sky that had ingulfed the telescope.

One of the tufts by which he held came out at the root, and Knight began to follow the quartz. It was a terrible moment. Elfride uttered a low wild wail of agony, bowed her head, and covered her face with her hands.

Between the turf-covered slope and the gigantic perpendicular rock intervened a weather-worn series of jagged edges, forming a face yet steeper than the former slope. As he slowly slid inch by inch upon these, Knight made a last desperate dash at the lowest tuft of vegetation—the last outlying knot of starved herbage ere the rock appeared in all its bareness. It arrested his farther descent. Knight was now literally suspended by his arms; but the incline of the brow being what engineers would call about a quarter in one, it was sufficient to relieve his arms of a portion of his weight, but was very far from offering an adequately flat face to support him.

In spite of this dreadful tension of body and mind Knight found time for a moment of thankfulness. Elfride was safe.

She lay on her side above him — her fingers clasped. Seeing him again steady, she jumped upon her feet.

'Now, if I can only save you by running for help!' she cried. 'O, I would have died instead! Why did you try so hard to deliver me?' And she turned away wildly to run for assistance.

'Elfride, how long will it take you to run to Endelstow and back?'

'Three-quarters of an hour.'

'That won't do; my hands will not hold out ten minutes. And is there nobody nearer?'

'No; unless a chance passer may happen to be.'

'He would have nothing with him that

could save me. Is there a pole or stick of any kind on the common?'

She gazed around. The common was bare of everything but heather and grass.

A minute — perhaps more time — was passed in mute thought by both. On a sudden the blank and helpless agony left her face. She vanished over the bank from his sight.

Knight felt himself in the presence of personalised loneliness.

CHAPTER IX.

'LOVE WILL FIND OUT THE WAY.'

HAGGARD cliffs, of every ugly altitude, are as common as sea-fowl along the line of coast between Exmoor and Land's End; but this outflanked and encompassed specimen was the ugliest of them all. Their summits are not safe places for scientific experiment on the principles of air-currents, as Knight had now found, to his dismay.

He still clutched the face of the escarpment — not with the frenzied hold of despair, but with a dogged determination to make the most of his every jot of endurance, and so give the longest possible scope to Elfride's intentions, whatever they might be.

He reclined hand in hand with the world in its infancy. Not a blade, not an insect, which spoke of the present, was between him and the past. The inveterate antagonism of these black precipices to all strugglers for life is in no way more forcibly suggested than by the absence of the minutest tufts of grass, lichens, or confervæ from their outermost ledges.

Knight pondered on the meaning of Elfride's hasty disappearance, but could not avoid an instinctive conclusion that there existed but a doubtful hope for him. As far as he could judge, his sole chance of deliverance lay in the possibility of a rope or pole being brought; and this possibility was remote indeed. The soil upon these high downs was left so untended that they were unenclosed for miles, except by a casual bank or dry wall, and were rarely visited but for the purpose of collecting or counting the flock which found a scanty means of subsistence thereon.

At first, when death appeared improbable, because it had never visited him before, Knight could think of no future, nor of anything connected with his past. He could only look sternly at Nature's treacherous attempt to put an end to him, and strive to thwart her.

From the fact that the cliff formed the inner face of the segment of a huge cylinder, having the sky for a top and the sea for a bottom, which enclosed the cove to the extent of more than a semicircle, he could see the vertical face curving round on each side of him. He looked far down the façade, and realised more thoroughly how it threatened him. Grimness was in every feature, and to its very bowels the inimical shape was desolation.

By one of those familiar conjunctions in which the inanimate world baits the mind of man when he pauses in moments of suspense, opposite Knight's eyes was an imbedded fossil, standing forth in low relief from the rock. It was a creature with eyes. The eyes, dead and turned to stone, were even now regarding him. It was one of the early crustaceans called Trilobites. Separated by millions of years in their lives, Knight and this underling seemed to have met in their death. It was the single instance within reach of his vision of anything that had ever been alive and had had a body to save, as he himself had now.

The creature represented but a low type of animal existence, for never in their vernal years had the plains indicated by those numberless slaty layers been traversed by an intelligence worthy of the name. Zoophytes, mollusca, shell-fish, were the highest developments of those ancient dates. The immense lapses of time each formation represented had known nothing of the dignity of man. They were grand times, but they were mean times too, and mean were their relics. He was to be with the small in his death.

Knight was a geologist; and such is the supremacy of habit over occasion, as a pioneer of the thoughts of men, that at this dreadful juncture his mind found time to take in, by a momentary sweep, the varied scenes that had had their day between this creature's epoch and his own. There is no place like a cleft landscape for bringing home such imaginings as these.

Time closed up like a fan before him. He saw himself at one extremity of the years, face to face with the beginning and all the intermediate centuries simultaneously. Fierce men, clothed in the hides of beasts, and carrying, for defence and attack, huge clubs and pointed spears, rose from the rock, like the phantoms before the doomed Macbeth. They lived in hollows, woods, and mud huts — perhaps in caves of the neighbouring rocks. Behind them stood an earlier band. No man was there. Huge elephantine forms, the mastodon, the hippopotamus, the tapir, antelopes of monstrous size, the megatherium, and the mylodon—all, for the moment, in juxtaposition. Farther back, and overlapped by these, were perched huge-billed birds and swinish creatures as large as horses. Still more shadowy were the sinister crocodilian outlines—alligators and other horrible reptiles, culminating in the colossal lizard, the iguanodon. Folded behind were dragon forms and clouds of flying reptiles: still underneath were fishy beings of lower development; and so on, till the life-time scenes of the fossil confronting him were a present and modern condition of things.

These images passed before Knight's inner eye in less than half a minute, and he was again considering the actual present. Was he to die? The mental picture of Elfride in the world, without himself to cherish her, smote his heart like a whip. He had hoped for deliverance, but what could a girl do? He dared not move an inch. Was Death really stretching out his hand? The previous sensation, that it was improbable he would die, was fainter now.

However, Knight still clung to the cliff.

To those hardy weather-beaten individuals who pass the greater part of their days and nights out-of-doors, Nature seems to have moods in other than a poetical sense: moods literally and really—predilections for certain deeds at certain times, without any apparent law to govern or season to account for them. They read her as a person with a curious temper. Thus: she does not scatter kindnesses and cruelties alternately, impartially, or in order—shining on them one day, raining on them the next—but heartless severities or overwhelming kindnesses in lawless caprice. Their case is always that of the prodigal's favourite or the miser's pensioner. In her unfriendly moments there seems a cruel fun in her tricks—a feline playfulness begotten by an anticipated pleasure in swallowing the victim.

This way of thinking had been absurd to Knight, but he began to adopt it now. He was first spitted on to a rock. New tortures followed after a while. The rain increased, and persecuted him with exceptional persistency, the reason of which he was moved to believe to be because he was in such a wretched state already. An entirely new order of things had been observed in this introduction of rain upon the scene. It rained upwards instead of down. The strong ascending current of air carried the rain-drops with it in its race up the escarpment, coming to him with such velocity that they stuck into his flesh like cold needles. Each drop was virtually a shaft, and it pierced him to his skin. These water-shafts seemed to lift him on their points: no downward rain ever had such a torturing effect. In a brief space he was drenched, except in two places. These were on the top of his shoulders and on the crown of his hat.

The wind, though not intense in other situations, was strong here. It tugged at his coat and lifted it. We are mostly accustomed to look upon all opposition which is not animate, as that of the stolid, inexorable hand of indifference, which wears out the patience more than the strength. Here, at any rate, hostility did not assume that slow sickening form. It was a cosmic agency, active, lashing, eager for conquest: determination; not an insensate standing in the way.

Knight had over-estimated the strength of his hands. They were getting weak already. 'She will never come again; she has been gone ten minutes,' he said to himself.

This mistake arose from the unusual compression of his experiences just now: she had really been gone but three.

'As many more minutes will be my end,' he thought.

Next came another instance of the incapacity of the mind to make comparisons at such times.

'This is a summer afternoon,' he said, 'and there can never have been such a heavy and cold rain on a summer day in my life before.'

He was again mistaken. The rain was quite ordinary in quantity; the air in temperature. It was, as is usual, the menacing attitude in which they approached him that magnified their powers.

He again looked straight downwards, the wind and the water-dashes lifting his moustache, scudding up his cheeks, under his eyelids, and into his eyes. This is what he saw down there: the surface of the sea —visually just past his toes, and under his feet; actually one-eighth of a mile, or more than two hundred yards, below them. We colour according to our moods the objects we survey. The sea would have been a deep neutral blue, had happier auspices attended the gazer: it was now no otherwise than distinctly black to his vision. That narrow white border was foam, he knew well; but its boisterous tosses were so distant as to appear a pulsation only, and its plashing was barely audible. A white border to a black sea—his funeral pall and its edging.

The world was to some extent turned upside down for him. Rain ascended from below. Beneath his feet was aerial space and the unknown; above him was the firm familiar ground, and upon it all that he loved best.

Pitiless Nature had then two voices, and two only. The nearer was the voice of the wind in his ears, rising and falling as it mauled and thrust him hard or softly. The second and distant one was the moan of that fathomless ocean below and afar— rubbing its restless flank against the Cliff without a Name.

Knight perseveringly held on. Had he any faith in Elfride? Perhaps. Love is faith, and faith, like a gathered flower, will live on a long time after nutriment has ceased.

Nobody would have expected the sun to shine on such an evening as this. Yet it appeared, low down upon the sea. Not with its natural golden fringe, sweeping the farthest ends of the landscape, not with the strange glare of whiteness which it sometimes puts on as an alternative with colour, but as a splotch of vermilion red upon a leaden ground—a red face looking on with a drunken leer.

Most men who have brains know it, and few are so foolish as to disguise this fact from themselves or others, even though an ostentatious display may be called self-conceit. Knight, without showing it much, knew that his intellect was above the average. And he thought—he could not help thinking—that his death would be a deliberate loss to earth of good material; that such an experiment in killing might have been practised upon some less developed life.

A fancy some people hold, when in a bitter mood, is that inexorable circumstance only tries to prevent what intelligence attempts. Renounce a desire for a long contested position, and go on another tack, and after a while the prize is thrown at you, seemingly in disappointment that no more tantalising is possible.

Knight gave up thoughts of life utterly and entirely, and turned to contemplate the Dark Valley and the unknown future beyond. Into the solemn depths of these reflections we will not pry. Let it suffice to state what followed.

At that moment of taking no more thought for this life, something disturbed the outline of the bank above him. A spot appeared.

It was the head of Elfride.

Knight immediately prepared to welcome life again.

The expression of a face consigned to utter loneliness, when a friend first looks in upon it, is moving in the extreme. In rowing seaward to a light-ship or sea-girt lighthouse, where, without any immediate terror of death, the inmates experience the gloom of monotonous seclusion, the grateful eloquence of their countenances at the greeting, expressive of thankfulness for the visit, is almost enough to stir the emotions of the observer.

Knight's upward look at Elfride was of a nature with, but far transcending, such an instance as this. The lines of his face had deepened to furrows, and every one of them thanked her visibly. His lips moved to the word 'Elfride,' though the motion evolved no sound. His eyes passed all description in their combination of the whole diapason of eloquence, from lover's deep love to fellow-man's gratitude for a token of remembrance from one of his kind.

Elfride had come back. What she had

come to do he did not know. She could only look on at his death, perhaps. Still, she had come back, and not deserted him utterly, and it was much.

It was a novelty in the extreme to see Henry Knight, to whom Elfride was but a child, who had swayed her as a tree sways a bird's-nest, who mastered her and made her weep most bitterly at her own insignificance, thus thankful for a sight of her face. She looked down upon him, her face glistening with rain and tears. He smiled faintly.

'How calm he is!' she thought. 'How great and noble he is to be so calm!' She would have died ten times for him then.

The gliding form of the steamboat caught her eye: she heeded it no longer.

'How much longer can you wait?' came from her pale lips and along the wind to his position.

'Four minutes,' said Knight, in a weaker voice than her own.

'But with a good hope of being saved?'

'Seven or eight.'

He now noticed that in her arms she bore a bundle of white linen, and that her form was singularly attenuated. So preternaturally thin and flexible was Elfride at this moment, that she appeared to bend under the light blows of the rain-shafts, as they struck into her sides and bosom, and splintered into spray on her face. There is nothing like a thorough drenching for reducing the protuberances of clothes, but Elfride's seemed to cling to her like a glove.

Without heeding the attack of the clouds further than by raising her hand and wiping away the spirts of rain when they went more particularly into her eyes, she sat down and hurriedly began rending the linen into strips. These she knotted end to end, and afterwards twisted them like the strands of a cord. In a short space of time she had formed a perfect rope by this means, six or seven yards long.

'Can you wait while I bind it?' she said, again anxiously extending her gaze down to him.

'Yes, if not very long. Hope has given me a wonderful instalment of strength.'

Elfride dropped her eyes again, tore the remaining material into narrow tape-like ligaments, knotted each to each as before, but on a smaller scale, and wound the lengthy string she had thus formed round and round the linen rope, which, without this binding, had a tendency to spread abroad.

'Now,' said Knight, who, watching the proceedings intently, had by this time not only grasped her scheme, but reasoned further on, 'I can hold three minutes longer yet. And do you use the time in testing the strength of the knots, one by one.'

She at once obeyed, tested each singly by putting her foot on the rope between each knot, and pulling with her hands. One of the knots slipped.

'O, think! It would have broken but for your forethought,' Elfride exclaimed apprehensively.

She re-tied the two ends. The rope was now firm in every part.

'When you have let it down,' said Knight, already resuming his position of ruling power, 'go back from the edge of the slope, and over the bank as far as the rope will allow you. Then lean down, and hold the end with both hands.'

He had first thought of a safer plan for his own deliverance, but it involved the disadvantage of possibly endangering her life.

'I have tied it round my waist,' she cried; 'and I will lean directly upon the bank, holding with my hands as well.'

It was the arrangement he had thought of, but would not suggest.

'I will raise and drop it three times when I am behind the bank,' she continued, 'to signify that I am ready. Take care, O, take the greatest care, I beg you!'

She dropped the rope over him, to learn how much of its length it would be necessary to expend on that side of the bank, went back, and disappeared as she had done before.

The rope was trailing by Knight's shoulders. In a few moments it moved three times.

He waited yet a second or two, then laid hold.

The incline of this upper portion of the precipice, to the length only of a few feet, useless to a climber empty-handed, was invaluable now. Not more than half his weight depended entirely on the linen rope. Half-a-dozen extensions of the arms, alternating with half-a-dozen seizures of the rope with his feet, brought him up to the level of the soil.

He was saved, and by Elfride.

He extended his cramped limbs like an

awakened sleeper, and sprang over the bank.

At sight of him she leapt to her feet with almost a shriek of joy. Knight's eyes met hers, and with supreme eloquence the glance of each told a long-concealed tale of emotion in that short half-moment. Moved by an impulse neither could resist, they ran together and into each other's arms.

At the moment of embracing, Elfride's eyes involuntarily flashed towards the *Puffin* steamboat. It had doubled the point, and was no longer to be seen.

An overwhelming rush of exultation at having delivered the man she revered from one of the most terrible forms of death, shook the gentle girl to the centre of her soul. It merged in a defiance of duty to Stephen, and a total recklessness as to plighted faith. Every nerve of her will was now in entire subjection to her feeling —volition as a guiding power had forsaken her. To remain passive, as she remained now, encircled by his arms, was a sufficiently complete result—a glorious crown to all the years of her life. Perhaps he was only grateful, and did not love her. No matter: it was infinitely more to be even the slave of the greater than the queen of the less. Some such sensation as this, though it was not recognised as a finished thought, raced along the impressible soul of Elfride.

Regarding their attitude, it was impossible for two persons to go nearer to a kiss than went Knight and Elfride during those minutes of impulsive embrace in the pelting rain. Yet they did not kiss. Knight's peculiarity of nature was such that it would not allow him to take advantage of the unguarded and passionate avowal she had tacitly made.

Elfride recovered herself, and gently struggled to be free.

He reluctantly relinquished her, and then surveyed her from crown to toe. She seemed as small as an infant. He perceived whence she had obtained the rope.

'Elfride, my Elfride!' he exclaimed in gratified amazement.

'I must leave you now,' she said, her face doubling its red, with an expression between gladness and shame. 'You follow me, but at some distance.'

'The rain and wind pierce you through; the chill will kill you. God bless you for such devotion! Take my coat and put it on.'

'No; I shall get warm running.'

Elfride had absolutely nothing between her and the weather but her exterior robe or 'costume.' The door had been made upon a woman's wit, and it had found its way out. Behind the bank, whilst Knight reclined upon the dizzy slope waiting for death, she had taken off her whole clothing, and replaced only her outer robe and skirt. Every thread of the remainder lay upon the ground in the form of a woollen and cotton rope.

'I am used to being wet through,' she added. 'I have been drenched on Pansy dozens of times. Good-bye till we meet, clothed and in our right minds, by the fireside at home!'

She then ran off from him through the pelting rain like a hare; or more like a pheasant when, scampering away with a lowered tail, it has a mind to fly, but does not. Elfride was soon out of sight.

Knight felt uncomfortably wet and chilled, but glowing with fervour nevertheless. He fully appreciated Elfride's girlish delicacy in refusing his escort in the meagre habiliments she wore, yet felt that necessary abstraction of herself for a short half-hour as a most grievous loss to him.

He gathered up her knotted and twisted plumage of linen, lace, and embroidery-work, and laid it across his arm. He noticed on the ground an envelope, limp and wet. In endeavouring to restore this to its proper shape, he loosened from the envelope a piece of paper it had contained, which was seized by the wind in falling from Knight's hand. It was blown to the right, blown to the left—it floated to the edge of the cliff and over the sea, where it was hurled aloft. It twirled in the air, and then flew back over his head.

Knight followed the paper, and secured it. Having done so, he looked to discover if it had been worth securing.

The troublesome sheet was a banker's receipt for two hundred pounds, placed to the credit of Miss Swancourt, which the impractical girl had totally forgotten she carried with her.

Knight folded it as carefully as its moist condition would allow, put it in his pocket, and followed Elfride.

CHAPTER X.

'SHOULD AULD ACQUAINTANCE BE FORGOT?'

By this time Stephen Smith had stepped out upon the quay at Stranton, and breathed his native air.

A darker skin, a more pronounced moustache, and an incipient beard, were the chief additions and changes noticeable in his appearance.

In spite of the falling rain, which had lessened somewhat, he took a small valise in his hand, and, leaving the remainder of his luggage at the inn, ascended the hills towards East Endelstow. This place lay in a vale of its own, farther inland than the west village, and though so near it, had little of physical feature in common with the latter. East Endelstow was more wooded and fertile: it boasted of Lord Luxellian's mansion and park, and was free from those bleak open uplands which lent such an air of desolation to the vicinage of the coast—always excepting the small valley in which stood the vicarage and Mrs. Swancourt's old house, the Crags.

Stephen had arrived nearly at the summit of the ridge, when the rain again increased its volume, and, looking about for temporary shelter, he ascended a steep path which penetrated dense hazel bushes in the lower part of its course. Farther up it emerged upon a ledge immediately over the turnpike-road, and sheltered by an overhanging face of rubble rock, with bushes above. For a reason of his own he made this spot his refuge from the storm, and turning his face to the left, conned the landscape as a book.

He was overlooking the valley containing Elfride's residence.

From this point of observation the prospect exhibited the peculiarity of being either brilliant foreground or the dark brown of distance, a sudden dip in the surface of the country lowering out of sight all the intermediate prospect. In apparent contact with the trees and bushes growing close beside him appeared the distant tract, terminated suddenly by the brink of the series of cliffs which culminated in the tall giant without a name—small and unimportant as here beheld. A leaf on a bough at Stephen's elbow blotted out a whole hill in the contrasting district far away; a green bunch of nuts covered a complete upland there, and the great cliff itself was outvied by a pigmy crag in the bank hard by him. Stephen had looked upon these things hundreds of times before to-day, but he had never viewed them with such tenderness as now.

Stepping forward in this direction yet a little farther, he could see the tower of West Endelstow church, beneath which he was to meet his Elfride that night. And at the same time he noticed, coming over the hill from the cliffs, a white speck in motion. It seemed first to be a sea-gull flying low, but ultimately proved to be a human figure, running with great rapidity. The form flitted on, heedless of the rain which had caused Stephen's halt in this place, dropped down the heathery hill, entered the vale, and was out of sight.

Whilst he meditated upon the meaning of this phenomenon, he was surprised to see swim into his ken from the same point of departure another moving speck, as different from the first as well could be, insomuch that it was perceptible only by its blackness. Slowly and regularly it took the same course, and there was not much doubt that this was the form of a man. He, too, gradually descended from the upper levels, and was lost in the valley below.

The rain had by this time again abated,

and Stephen returned to the road. Looking ahead he saw two men and a cart. They were soon obscured by the intervention of a high hedge. Just before they emerged again he heard voices in conversation.

''A must soon be in the naibourhood, too, if so be he's a-coming,' said a tenor tongue, which Stephen instantly recognised as Martin Cannister's.

''A must 'a b'lieve,' said another voice— that of Stephen's father.

Stephen stepped forward, and came before them face to face. His father and Martin were walking, dressed in their second-best suits, and beside them rambled along a grizzel horse and brightly-painted spring-cart.

'All right, Mr. Cannister; here's the lost man!' exclaimed young Smith, entering at once upon the old style of greeting. 'Father, here I am.'

'All right, my sonny; and glad I be

for't!' returned John Smith, overjoyed to see the young man. 'How be ye? Well, come along home, and don't let's bide out here in the damp. Such weather must be terrible bad for a young chap just come from a fiery nation like Indy; hey, naibour Cannister?'

'Trew, trew. And about getting home his traps? Boxes, monstrous bales, and noble packages of foreign description, I make no doubt?'

'Hardly all that,' said Stephen, laughing.

'We brought the cart, maning to go right on to Stranton afore ye landed,' said his father. '"Put in the horse," says Martin. "Ay," says I, "so we will;" and did it straightway. Now, maybe, Martin had better go on wi' the cart for the things, and you and I walk home-along.'

'And I shall be back a'most as soon as you. Peggy is a pretty step still, though time d' begin to tell upon her as upon the rest o' us.'

Stephen told Martin where to find his baggage, and then continued his journey homeward in the company of his father.

'Owing to your coming a day sooner than we first expected,' said John, 'you'll find us in a turk of a mess, sir—"sir," says I to my own son! but ye've gone up so, Stephen. We've killed the pig this morning for ye, thinking ye'd be hungry, and glad of a morsel of fresh mate. And 'a won't be cut up till to-night. However, we can make ye a good supper of fry, which will chaw up well wi' a dab o' mustard and a few nice new taters, and a drop of shilling ale to wash it down. Your mother have scrubbed the house through because ye were coming, and dusted all the chimmer furniture, and bought a new basin and jug of a travelling crockery-woman that came to our door, and scoured the cannelsticks, and claned the winders! Ay, I don't know what 'a ha'n't a done. Never wer such a steer, 'a b'lieve.'

Conversation of this kind and inquiries of Stephen for his mother's well-being occupied them for the remainder of the journey. When they drew near the river, and the cottage behind it, they could hear the master-mason's clock striking off the bygone hours of the day at intervals of a quarter of a minute, during which intervals Stephen's imagination readily pictured his mother's forefinger wandering round the dial in company with the minute-hand.

'The clock stopped this morning, and your mother is putting en right seemingly,' said his father in an explanatory tone; and they went up the garden to the door.

When they had entered, and Stephen had dutifully and warmly greeted his mother—who appeared in a cotton dress of a dark-blue ground, covered broadcast with a multitude of new and full moons, stars, and planets, with an occasional dash of a comet-like aspect to diversify the scene — the crackle of cart-wheels was heard outside, and Martin Cannister stamped in at the doorway, in the form of a pair of legs beneath a great box, his body being nowhere visible. When the luggage had been all taken down, and Stephen had gone up-stairs to change his clothes, Mrs. Smith's mind seemed to recover a lost thread.

'Really our clock is not worth a penny,' she said, turning to it and attempting to start the pendulum.

'Stopped again?' inquired Martin with commiseration.

'Yes, sure,' replied Mrs. Smith; and continued after the manner of certain matrons, to whose tongues the harmony of a subject with a casual mood is a greater recommendation than its pertinence to the occasion, 'John would spend pounds a year upon the jimcrack old thing, if he might, in having it claned, when at the same time you may doctor it yourself as well. "The clock's stopped again, John,"

I say to him. "Better have en claned," says he. There's five shillings. "That clock grinds again," I say to en. "Better have en claned," 'a says again. "That clock strikes wrong, John," says I. "Better have en claned," he goes on. The wheels would have been polished to skeletons by this time if I had listened to en, and I assure you we could have bought a chainey-faced beauty wi' the good money we've flung away these last ten years upon this old green-faced mortal. And, Martin, you must be wet. My son is gone up to change. John is damper than I should like to be, but 'a calls it nothing. Some of Mrs. Swancourt's servants have been here—they ran in out of the rain when going for a walk—and I assure you the state of bonnets was frightful—'

'How's the folks? We've been over to Stranton, and what wi' running and stopping out of the storms, my poor head is beyond everything! fizz, fizz, fizz; 'tis frying o' fish from morning to night,' said a cracked voice in the doorway at this instant.

'Lord so's, who's that?' said Mrs. Smith, in a private exclamation, and turning round saw William Worm, endeavouring to make himself look passing civil and friendly by overspreading his face with a large smile that seemed to have no connection with the humour he was in. Behind him stood a woman about twice his size, with a large umbrella over her head. This was Mrs. Worm, William's wife.

'Come in, William,' said John Smith. 'We don't kill a pig every day. And you likewise, Mrs. Worm. I make ye welcome. Since ye left Parson Swancourt, William, I don't see much of ye.'

'No, for to tell the truth, since I took to the turnpike-gate line, I've been out but little, coming to church o' Sundays not being my duty now, as 'twas in a parson's family, you see. However, our boy is able to mind the gate now, and I said, says I. "Barbara, let's call and see John Smith."'

'I am sorry to hear yer pore head is so bad still.'

'Ay, I assure you that frying o' fish is going on for nights and days. And, you know, sometimes 'tisn't only fish, but rashers o' bacon and inions. Ay, I can hear the fat pop and fizz as nateral as life; can't I, Barbara?'

Mrs. Worm, who had been all this time engaged in closing her umbrella, corroborated this statement, and now, coming indoors, showed herself to be a wide-faced, comfortable-looking woman, with a wart upon her cheek, bearing a small tuft of hair in its centre.

'Have ye ever tried anything to cure yer noise, Master Worm?' inquired Martin Cannister.

'O ay; bless ye, I've tried everything. Ay, Providence is a merciful man, and I have hoped he'd have found it out by this time, living so many years in a parson's family, too, as I have, but 'a don't seem to relieve me. Ay, I be a poor wambling man, and life's a mere bubble.'

'True, mournful true, William Worm. 'Tis so. The world wants looking to, or 'tis all sixes and sevens wi' us.'

'Take your things off, Mrs. Worm,' said Mrs. Smith. 'We be rather in a muddle, to tell the truth, for my son is jist dropped in from Indy a day sooner than we expected, and the pig-killer is coming presently to cut up.'

Mrs. Barbara Worm, not wishing to take any mean advantage of persons in a muddle by observing them, removed her bonnet and mantle with eyes fixed upon the flowers in the plot outside the door.

'What beautiful tiger-lilies!' said Mrs. Worm.

'Yes, they be very well, but such a trouble to me on account of the children that come here. They will go eating the berries on the stem, and call 'em currants. Taste wi' junivals is quite fancy, really.'

'And your snapdragons look as fierce as ever.'

'Well, really,' answered Mrs. Smith, entering didactically into the subject, 'they are more like Christians than flowers. But they make up well enough wi' the rest, and don't require much tending. And the same can be said o' these miller's wheels. 'Tis a flower I like very much, though so simple. Having them is like asking your relations to a party—they count up for a show, and you haven't the trouble of complimenting 'em. John says he'd never care about the flowers o' 'em, but men have no eye for anything nate. He says his favourite flower is a cauliflower. And I assure you I tremble in the spring-time, for 'tis perfect murder.'

'You don't say so, Mrs. Smith!'

'John digs round the roots, you know.

In goes his blundering spade, through roots, bulbs, everything that hasn't got a good show above ground, turning 'em up cut all to slices. Only the very last fall I went to move some tulips, when I found every bulb upside down, and the stems crooked round. He had turned 'em over in the spring, and the cunning creatures had soon found that heaven was not where it used to be.'

'What's that long-favoured flower under the hedge?'

'They? O Lord, they are the horrid Jacob's ladders! Instead of praising 'em, I be mad wi' 'em for being so ready to bide where they are not wanted. They be very well in their way, but I do not care for things that neglect won't kill. Do what I will, dig, drag, scrap, pull, I get too many of 'em. I chop the roots: up they'll come, treble strong. Throw 'em over hedge; there they'll grow, staring me in the face like a hungry dog drove away, and creep back again in a week or two the same as before. 'Tis Jacob's ladder here, Jacob's ladder there, and plant 'em where nothing in the world will grow, you get crowds of 'em in a month or two. John made a new manure mixen last summer, and he said, " Mariar, now if you've got any flowers or such like, that you don't want, you may plant 'em round my mixen so as to hide it a bit, though 'tis not likely anything of much value will grow there." I thought, "There's them Jacob's ladders; I'll put them there, since they can't do harm in sich a place;" and I planted the Jacob's ladders sure enough. They growed, and they growed, in the mixen and out of the mixen, all over the litter, covering it quite up. When John wanted to use it about the garden, 'a said, " Nation seize them Jacob's ladders of yours, Mariar! They've eat the goodness out of every morsel of my manure, so that 'tis no better than sand itself!" Sure enough the hungry mortels had. 'Tis my belief that in the secret souls o' 'em, Jacob's ladders be weeds, and not flowers at all, if the truth was known.'

Robert Lickpan, pig-killer and carrier, arrived at this moment. The fatted animal hanging in the back kitchen was cleft down the middle of its backbone, Mrs. Smith being meanwhile engaged in cooking supper.

Between the cutting and chopping, ale was handed round, and Worm and the pig-killer listened to John Smith's description of the meeting with Stephen, with eyes blankly fixed upon the table-cloth, in order that nothing in the external world should interrupt their efforts to conjure up the scene correctly:

Stephen came down-stairs in the middle of the story, and after the little interruption occasioned by his entrance and welcome, the narrative was again continued, precisely as if he had not been there at all, and was told inclusively to him, as to somebody who knew nothing about the matter.

'"Ay," I said, as I catched sight o' en through the brimbles, "that's the lad, for I d' know en by his grandfather's walk;" for 'a stapped out like poor father for all the world. Still there was a touch o' the frisky that set me wondering. 'A got closer, and I said, "That's the lad, for I d' know en by his carrying a black case like a travelling man." Still, a road is common to all the world, and there be more travelling men than one. But I kept my eye cocked, and I said to Martin, "'Tis the boy, now, for I d' know en by the wold twirl o' the stick and the family step." Then 'a cam closer, and 'a said, "All right." I could swear to en then.'

Stephen's personal appearance was next criticised.

'He d' look a deal thinner in face, surely, than when I seed en at the parson's, and never knowed en, if ye'll believe me,' said Martin.

'Ay, there,' said another, without removing his eyes from Stephen's face, 'I should ha' knowed en anywhere. 'Tis his father's nose to a T.'

'It has been often remarked,' said Stephen modestly.

'And he's certainly taller,' said Martin, letting his glance run over Stephen's form from bottom to top.

'I was thinking 'a was exactly the same height,' Worm replied.

'Bless thy soul, that's because he's bigger round likewise.' And the united eyes all moved to Stephen's waist.

'I be a poor wambling man, but I can make allowances,' said William Worm. 'Ah, sure, and how he cam as a stranger and pilgrim to Parson Swancourt's that time, not a soul knowing en after so many years! Ay, life's a strange bubble, Stephen: but I suppose I must say Sir to ye?'

'O, it is not necessary at present,' Stephen replied, though mentally resolving to avoid the vicinity of these familiar friends as soon as he had made pretensions to the hand of Elfride.

'Ah, well,' said Worm musingly, 'some would have looked for no less than a Sir. There's a sight of difference in people.'

'And in pigs likewise,' observed John Smith, looking at the halved carcass of his own.

Robert Lickpan, the pig-killer, here seemed called upon to enter the lists of conversation.

'Yes, they've got their particular naters good-now,' he remarked initially. 'Many's the rum-tempered pig I've knowed.'

'I don't doubt it, Master Lickpan,' answered Martin, in a tone expressing that his convictions, no less than good manners, demanded the reply.

'Yes,' continued the pig-killer, as one accustomed to be heard. 'One that I knowed was deaf and dumb, and we couldn't make out what was the matter wi' the pig. 'A would eat well enough when a' seed the trough, but when his back was turned, you might a-rattled the bucket all day, the poor soul never heard ye. Ye could play tricks upon en behind his back, and 'a wouldn't find it out no quicker than poor deaf Grammer Cates. But 'a fatted well, and I never seed a pig open better when 'a was killed, and 'a was very tender eating, very; as pretty a bit of mate as ever you see; you could suck that mate through a quill.

'And another I knowed,' resumed the killer, after quietly letting a pint of ale run down his throat of its own accord, and setting down the cup with mathematical exactness upon the spot from which he had raised it—'another went out of his mind.'

'How very mournful!' murmured Mrs. Worm.

'Ay, poor thing, 'a did! As clean out of his mind as the cleverest Christian could go. In early life 'a was very melancholy, and never seemed a hopeful pig by no means. 'Twas Andrew Candle's pig—that's whose pig 'twas.'

'I can mind the pig well enough,' attested John Smith.

'And a pretty little porker 'a was. And you all know Farmer Buckle's sort? Every jack o' 'em suffer from the rheumatism to this day, owing to a damp sty they lived in when they were striplings, as 'twere.'

'Well, now we'll weigh,' said John.

'If so be he were not so fine, we'd weigh en whole: but as he is, we'll take a side at a time. John, you can mind my old joke, ey? A good old joke, that.'

'I do so; though 'twas a good few years ago I first heard en.'

'Yes,' said Lickpan, 'that there old familiar joke have been in our family for generations, I may say. My father used that joke constantly at pig-killings for more than five-and-forty years—the time he followed the calling. And 'a told me that 'a had it from his father when he was quite a chiel, who made use o' en just the same at every killing more or less; and pig-killings were pig-killings in those days.'

'Trewly they were.'

'I've never heard the joke,' said Mrs. Smith tentatively.

'Nor I,' chimed in Mrs. Worm, who, being the only other lady in the room, felt bound by the laws of courtesy to feel like Mrs. Smith in everything.

'Surely, surely you have,' said the killer, looking sceptically at the benighted females. 'However, 'tisn't much—I don't wish to say it is. It commences like this: "Bob will tell the weight of your pig, 'a b'lieve," says I. The congregation of neighbours think I mane my son Bob, naturally; but the secret is that I mane the bob o' the steelyard. Ha, ha, ha!'

'Haw, haw, haw!' laughed Martin Cannister, who had heard the explanation of this striking story for the hundredth time.

'Huh, huh, huh!' laughed John Smith. who had heard it for the thousandth.

'Hee, hee, hee!' laughed William Worm, who had never heard it at all, but was afraid to say so.

'Thy grandfather, Robert, must have been a wide-awake chap to make that story,' said Martin Cannister, subsiding to a placid aspect of delighted criticism.

'He had a head, by all account. And, you see, as the first-born of the Lickpans have all been Roberts, they've all been Bobs, so the story was handed down to the present day.'

'Poor Joseph, your second boy, will never be able to bring it out in company, which is rather unfortunate,' said Mrs. Worm thoughtfully.

"'A wont. Yes, grandfer was a clever chap, as ye say; but I knowed a cleverer. 'Twas my uncle Levi. Uncle Levi made a snuff-box that should be a puzzle to his friends to open. He used to hand en round at wedding parties, christenings, funerals, and in other jolly company, and let 'em try their skill. This extraordinary snuff-box had a spring behind that would push in and out—a hinge where seemed to be the cover; a slide at the end, a screw in front, and knobs and mysterious notches everywhere. One man would try the spring, another would try the screw, another would try the slide; but try as they would, the box wouldn't open. And they couldn't open en, and they didn't open en. Now what might you think was the secret of that box?'

All put on an expression that their united thoughts were inadequate to the occasion.

'Why, the box wouldn't open at all.

'A were made not to open, and ye might have tried till the end of Revelations, 'twould have been as naught, for the box were glued all round.'

'A very deep man to have made such a box.'

'Yes. 'Twas like uncle Levi all over.'

''Twas. I can mind the man very well. Tallest man ever I seed.'

''A was so. He never slept upon a bedstead after he growed up a hard boy-chap—never could get one long enough. When 'a lived in that little small house by the pond, he used to have to leave open his chamber door every night at going to bed, and let his feet poke out upon the landing.'

'He's dead and gone now, nevertheless, poor man, as we all shall,' observed Worm, to fill the pause which followed the conclusion of Robert Lickpan's speech.

The weighing and cutting up was pursued amid an animated discourse on Stephen's travels; and at the finish, the first-fruits of the day's slaughter, fried in onions, were then turned from the pan into a dish on the table, each piece steaming and frizzling till it reached their very mouths.

It must be owned that the gentlemanly son of the house looked rather out of place in the course of this operation. Nor was his mind quite philosophic enough to allow him to be comfortable with these old-established persons, his father's friends. He had never lived long at home—scarcely at all since his childhood. The presence of William Worm was the most awkward feature of the case, for, though Worm had left the house of Mr. Swancourt, the being hand in glove with a *ci-devant* servitor reminded Stephen too forcibly of the vicar's classification of himself before he went from England. Mrs. Smith was conscious of the defect in her arrangements which had brought about the undesired conjunction. She spoke to Stephen privately.

'I am above having sich people here, Stephen; but what could I do? And your father is so rough in his nature that he's more mixed up with 'em than need be.'

'Never mind, mother,' said Stephen; 'I'll put up with it now.'

'When we leave my lord's service, and get farther down the country—as I hope we shall soon — it will be different. We shall be among fresh people, and in a larger house, and shall keep ourselves up a bit, I hope.'

'Is Miss Swancourt at home, do you know?' Stephen inquired.

'Yes, your father saw her this morning.'

'Do you often see her?'

'Scarcely ever. Mr. Glim, the curate, calls occasionally, but the Swancourts don't come into the village now any more than to drive through it. They dine at my lord's oftener than they used. Ah, here's a note was brought this morning for you by a boy.'

Stephen eagerly took the note and opened it, his mother watching him. He read what Elfride had written and sent before she started for the cliff that afternoon:

'Yes; I will meet you in the church at nine to-night.—E. S.'

'I don't know, Stephen,' his mother said meaningly, 'whe'r you still think about Miss Elfride, but if I were you I wouldn't concern about her. They say that none of old Mrs. Swancourt's money will come to her stepdaughter.'

'I see the evening has turned out fine; I am going out for a little while to look round the place,' he said, evading the direct query. 'Probably by the time I return our visitors will be gone, and we'll have a more confidential talk.'

CHAPTER XI.

'BREEZE, BIRD, AND FLOWER CONFESS THE HOUR.'

The rain had ceased since the sunset, but it was a cloudy night; and the light of the moon, softened and dispersed by its misty veil, was distributed over the land in pale gray.

A dark figure stepped from the doorway of John Smith's river-side cottage, and strode rapidly towards West Endelstow with a light footstep. Soon ascending from the lower levels he turned a corner, followed a cart-track, and saw the tower of the church he was in quest of distinctly shaped forth against the sky. In less than half an hour from the time of starting he swung himself over the churchyard stile.

The wild irregular enclosure was as much as ever an integral part of the old hill. The grass was still long, the graves were shaped precisely as passing years chose to alter them from their orthodox form as laid down by Martin Cannister, and by Stephen's own grandfather before him.

A sound sped into the air from the direction in which Stranton lay. It was the striking of the church clock, distinct in the still atmosphere as if it had come from the tower hard by, which, wrapt in its solitary silentness, gave out no such sounds of life.

'One, two, three, four, five, six, seven, eight, nine.' Stephen carefully counted the strokes, though he well knew their number beforehand. Nine o'clock. It was the hour Elfride had herself named as the most convenient for meeting him.

Stephen stood at the door of the porch and listened. He could have heard the softest breathing of any person within the porch; nobody was there. He went inside the doorway, sat down upon the stone bench, and waited with a beating heart.

The faint sounds heard only accented the silence. The rising and falling of the sea, far away along the coast, was the most important. A minor sound was the scurr of a distant night-hawk. Among the minutest where all were minute were the light settlement of gossamer fragments floating in the air, a toad humbly labouring along through the grass near the entrance, the crackle of a dead leaf which a worm was endeavouring to pull into the earth, a waft of air, getting nearer and nearer, and expiring at his feet under the burden of a winged seed.

Among all these soft sounds came not the only soft sound he cared to hear—the footfall of Elfride.

For a whole quarter of an hour Stephen sat thus intent, without moving a muscle.

At the end of that time he walked to the west front of the church. Turning the corner of the tower, a white form stared him in the face. He started back, and recovered himself. It was the tomb of young farmer Jethway, looking still as fresh and as new as when it was first erected, the white stone in which it was hewn having a singular weirdness amid the dark blue slabs from local quarries, of which the whole remaining gravestones were formed.

He thought of the night when he had sat thereon with Elfride as his companion, and well remembered his regret that she had received, even unwillingly, earlier homage than his own. But his present tangible anxiety reduced such a feeling to sentimental nonsense in comparison; and he strolled on over the graves to the border of the churchyard, whence in the daytime could be clearly seen the vicarage and the present residence of the Swancourts. No footstep was discernible upon the path up the hill, but a light was shining from a window in the last-named house.

Stephen knew there could be no mistake about the time or place, and no difficulty about keeping the engagement. He waited yet longer, passing from impatience into a mood which failed to take any account of the lapse of time. He was awakened from his reverie by Stranton clock.

One, two, three, four, five, six, seven, eight, nine, TEN.

One little fall of the hammer in addition to the number it had been sharp pleasure to hear, and what a difference to him!

He left the churchyard on the side opposite to his point of entrance, and went down the hill. Slowly he drew near the gate of her house. This he softly opened, and walked up the gravel drive to the door. Here he paused for several minutes.

At the expiration of that time the murmured speech of a manly voice came out to his ears through an open window behind the corner of the house. This was responded to by a clear soft laugh. It was the laugh of Elfride.

Stephen was conscious of a gnawing pain at his heart. He retreated as he had come. There are disappointments which wring us, and there are those which inflict a wound whose mark we bear to our graves. Such are so keen that no future gratification of the same desire can ever obliterate them: they become registered at once as a permanent loss of happiness. Such a one was Stephen's now: the crowning aureola of the dream had been the meeting here by stealth; and if Elfride had come to him only ten minutes after he had turned away, the disappointment would have been recognisable still.

When the young man reached home, he found there a letter which had arrived in his absence. Believing it to contain some reason for her non-appearance, yet unable to imagine one that could justify her, he hastily tore open the envelope.

The paper contained not a word from Elfride. It was the deposit-note for his two hundred pounds. On the back was the form of a cheque, and this she had filled up with the same sum, payable to the bearer.

Stephen was confounded. He attempted to divine her motive. Considering how limited was his knowledge of her later actions, he guessed rather shrewdly that, between the time of her sending the note in the morning and the evening's silent refusal of his gift, something had occurred which had caused a total change in her attitude towards him.

He knew not what to do. It seemed absurd now to go to her father next morning, as he had purposed, and ask for an engagement with her, a possibility impending all the while that Elfride herself would not be on his side. Only one course recommended itself as wise. To wait and see what the days would bring forth; to go and execute his commissions in Birmingham; then to return, learn if anything had transpired, and try what a meeting might do: perhaps her surprise at his backwardness would bring her forward to show latent warmth as decidedly as in old times.

This act of patience was in keeping only with the nature of a man precisely of Stephen's constitution. Nine men out of ten would perhaps have rushed off, got into her presence by fair means or foul, and provoked a catastrophe of some sort. Possibly for the better, probably for the worse.

He started for Birmingham the next morning. A day's delay would have made no difference; but he could not rest until he had begun and ended the programme proposed to himself. Bodily activity will sometimes take the sting out of anxiety as completely as assurance itself.

CHAPTER XII.

'MINE OWN FAMILIAR FRIEND.'

DURING these days of absence Stephen lived under alternate conditions. Whenever his emotions were active, he was in agony. Whenever he was not in agony, the business in hand had driven out of his mind by sheer force all deep reflection on the subject of Elfride and love.

By the time he commenced his return journey at the week's end, Stephen had very nearly worked himself up to an intention to call and see her face to face. On this occasion also he adopted his favourite route—by steamer from Bristol to Stranton; the time saved by speed on the railway being wasted at junctions, and in following a devious course.

It was a bright silent evening at the beginning of September when Smith again set foot in the little town. He felt inclined to linger a while upon the quay before ascending the hills, having formed a romantic intention to go home by way of her house, yet not wishing to wander in its neighbourhood till the evening shades should sufficiently screen him from observation.

And thus waiting for night's nearer approach, he watched the placid scene, over which the pale luminosity of the west cast a sorrowful monochrome, that became slowly embrowned by the dusk. A star appeared, and another, and another. They sparkled amid the yards and rigging of the two coal brigs lying alongside, as if they had been tiny lamps suspended in the ropes. The masts rocked sleepily to the infinitesimal flux of the tide, which clucked and gurgled with idle regularity in nooks and holes of the harbour wall.

The twilight was now quite pronounced enough for his purpose; and as, rather sad at heart, he was about to move on, a little boat containing two persons glided up the middle of the harbour with the lightness of a shadow. The boat came opposite him, passed on, and touched the landing-steps at the farther end. One of its occupants was a man, as Stephen had known by the easy stroke of the oars. When the pair ascended the steps, and came into greater prominence, he was enabled to discern that the second personage was a female; also that she wore a white decoration—apparently a feather—in her hat or bonnet, which spot of white was the only distinctly visible portion of her clothing.

Stephen remained a moment in their rear, and they passed on, when he pursued his way also, and soon forgot the circumstance. Having crossed a bridge, forsaken the high-road, and entered the footpath which led up the vale to West Endelstow, he heard a little wicket click softly together some yards ahead. By the time Stephen had reached the wicket and passed it, he heard another click of precisely the same nature from another gate yet farther on. Clearly some person or persons were preceding him along the path, their footsteps being rendered noiseless by the soft carpet of turf. Stephen now walked a little quicker, and perceived two forms. One of them bore aloft the white feather he had noticed in the female's hat on the quay: they were the couple he had seen in the boat. Stephen dropped a little farther to the rear.

From the bottom of the valley, along which the path had hitherto lain, beside the margin of the trickling streamlet, another path now diverged, and ascended the slope of the left-hand hill. This footway led only to the residence of Mrs. Swancourt and a cottage or two in its vicinity. No grass covered this diverging path in portions of its length, and Stephen was reminded that the pair in front of him had taken this route by the occasional rattle of loose stones under their feet. Stephen climbed in the same direction, but for some undefined reason he trod more softly than did those preceding him. His mind was unconsciously in exercise upon whom the female might be—whether a visitor to the Crags, a servant, or Elfride. He put it to himself yet more forcibly; could the lady be Elfride? A possible reason for her unaccountable failure to keep the appointment with him returned with painful force.

They entered the grounds of the house by the side wicket, whence the path, now wide and well trimmed, wended fantastically through the shrubbery to an octagonal pavilion called the Belvedere, by reason of the comprehensive view over the adjacent district that its green seats afforded. The path passed this erection and went on to the house as well as to the gardener's cottage on the other side, straggling thence to East Endelstow; so that Stephen felt no hesitation in entering a promenade which could scarcely be called private.

He fancied he heard the gate open and swing together again behind him. Turning, he saw nobody.

The people of the boat came to the summer-house. One of them spoke.

'I am afraid we shall get a scolding for being so late.'

Stephen instantly recognised the familiar voice, richer and fuller now than it used to be. 'Elfride!' he whispered to himself, and held fast by a sapling, to steady himself under the agitation her presence caused him. His heart swerved from its beat; he shunned having the meaning he sought.

'A breeze is rising again; how the ash-tree rustles!' said Elfride. 'Don't you hear it? I wonder what the time is.'

Stephen relinquished the sapling.

'I will get a light and tell you. Step into the summer-house; the air is quiet there.'

The cadence of that voice—he seemed to recognise its peculiarity, as he had recognised some notes of the northern birds on his return to his native clime, as an old natural thing renewed, yet not particularly noticed as natural before that renewal.

They entered the Belvedere. In the lower part it was formed of close woodwork nailed crosswise, and had openings in the upper by way of windows.

The scratch of a striking light was heard, and a bright glow radiated from the interior of the building. The light was the mother of a thousand new existences. It gave birth to dancing leaf-shadows, stem-shadows, lustrous streaks, dots, sparkles, and threads of silver sheen of all imaginable variety and transience. It awakened gnats, which flew towards it, revealed shiny gossamer threads, disturbed earthworms. Stephen gave but little attention to these phenomena, and less time. He saw in the summer-house a strongly-illuminated picture.

First, the face of his friend and preceptor Henry Knight, between whom and himself an estrangement had arisen, not from any definite causes beyond those of absence, increasing age, and diverging sympathies.

Next, his bright particular star, Elfride. The face of Elfride was more womanly than when she had called herself his, but as clear and healthy as ever. Her plenteous twines of beautiful hair were looking much as usual, with the exception of a slight modification in their arrangement, in deference to the changes of fashion.

Their two foreheads were close together, almost touching, and both were looking down. Elfride was holding her watch, Knight was holding the light with one hand, his left arm being round her waist.

Part of the scene reached Stephen's eyes through the horizontal bars of woodwork, which crossed their forms like the ribs of a skeleton.

Knight's arm stole still farther round the waist of Elfride.

'It is half-past eight,' she said in a low voice, which had a peculiar music in it, seemingly born of a thrill of pleasure at the new proof that she was beloved.

The flame dwindled down, died away, and all was wrapped in a darkness to which the gloom before the illumination bore no comparison in apparent density. Stephen, shattered in spirit and sick to his heart's centre, turned away. In turning, he saw a shadowy outline behind the summer-house on the other side. His eyes grew accustomed to the darkness. Was the form a human form, or was it an opaque bush of juniper?

The lovers arose, brushed against the laurestines, and pursued their way to the house. The indistinct figure had moved, and now passed across Smith's front. So completely enveloped was the person, that it was impossible to recognise him or her any more than as a shape. The shape glided noiselessly on.

Stephen stepped forward, fearing any mischief was intended to the other two. 'Who are you?' he said.

'Never mind who I am,' answered a weak whisper from the enveloping folds. '*What* I am, may she be! Perhaps I knew well—ah, so well!—a youth whose place you took, as he there now takes yours. Will you let her break your heart, and bring you to an untimely grave, as she did the one before you?'

'You are Mrs. Jethway, I think. What do you do here? And why do you talk so wildly?'

'Because my heart is desolate, and nobody cares about it. May hers be so that brought trouble upon me!'

'Silence!' said Stephen, staunch to Elfride in spite of himself. 'She would harm nobody wilfully, never would she! How do you come here?'

'I saw the two coming up the path, and wanted to learn if she were not one of them. Can I help disliking her if I think of the past? Can I help watching her if I remember my boy? Can I help ill-wishing her if I well-wish him?'

The bowed form went on, passed through the wicket, and was enveloped by the shadows of the field.

Stephen had heard that Mrs. Jethway, since the death of her son, had become a crazed, forlorn woman; and bestowing a pitying thought upon her, he dismissed her fancied wrongs from his mind, but not her condemnation of Elfride's faithlessness. That entered into and mingled with the sensations his new experience had begotten. The tale told by the little scene he had witnessed ran parallel with the unhappy woman's opinion, which, however baseless it might have been antecedently, had become true enough as regarded himself.

A slow weight of despair, as distinct from a violent paroxysm as starvation from a mortal shot, filled him and wrung him body and soul. The discovery had not been altogether unexpected, for throughout his anxiety of the last few days since the night in the churchyard, he had been inclined to construe the uncertainty unfavourably for himself. His hopes for the best had been but periodic interruptions of a chronic fear of the worst.

A strange concomitant of his misery was the singularity of its form. That his rival should be Knight, whom once upon a time he had adored as a man is very rarely adored by another in modern times, and whom he loved now, added deprecation to sorrow, and cynicism to both. Henry Knight, whose praises he had so frequently trumpeted in her ears, of whom she had actually been jealous, lest she herself should be lessened in Stephen's love on account of him, had probably won her the more easily by reason of those very praises which he had only ceased to utter by her command. She had ruled him like a queen in that matter, as in all others. Stephen could tell by her manner, brief as had been his observation of it, and by her words, few as they were, that her position was far different with Knight. That she looked up at and adored her new lover from below his pedestal, was even more perceptible than that she had smiled down upon Stephen from a height above him.

The suddenness of Elfride's renunciation of himself was food for more torture. To an unimpassioned outsider, it admitted of at least two interpretations—it might either have proceeded from an endeavour to be faithful to her first choice, till the lover seen absolutely overpowered the lover remembered, or from a wish not to lose his love till sure of the love of another. But to Stephen Smith the motive involved in the latter alternative made it untenable where Elfride was the actor.

He mused on her letters to him, in which she had never mentioned a syllable concerning Knight. It is desirable, however, to observe that only in two letters could she possibly have done so. One was written about a week before Knight's arrival, when, though she did not mention his promised coming to Stephen, she had hardly a definite reason in her mind for neglecting to do it. In the next she did casually allude to Knight. But Stephen had left Bombay long before that letter arrived.

Stephen looked at the black form of the adjacent house, where it cut a dark polygonal notch out of the sky, and felt that he hated the spot. He did not know many facts of the case, but could not help instinctively associating Elfride's fickleness with the marriage of her father and their introduction to London society. He closed the iron gate bounding the shrubbery as noiselessly as he had opened it, and went into the grassy field. Here he could see the old vicarage, the house alone that was associated with the sweet pleasant time of his incipient love for Elfride. Turning sadly from the place that was no longer a nook in which his thoughts might nestle when he was far away, he wandered in the direction of the east village, to reach his father's house before they retired to rest.

The nearest way to the cottage was by crossing the park. He did not hurry. Happiness frequently has reason for haste, but it is seldom that desolation need scramble or strain. Sometimes he paused under the low-hanging arms of the trees, looking vacantly on the ground.

Stephen was standing thus, scarcely

less crippled in thought than he was blank in vision, when a clear sound permeated the quiet air about him, and spread on far beyond. The sound was the stroke of a bell from the tower of East Endelstow church, which stood in a dell not forty yards from Lord Luxellian's mansion, and within the park enclosure. Another stroke greeted his ear, and gave character to both: then came a slow succession of them.

'Somebody is dead,' he said aloud.

The death knell of an inhabitant of the eastern parish was being tolled.

An unusual feature in the tolling was that it had not been begun according to the custom in Endelstow and other parishes in the neighbourhood. At every death the sex and age of the deceased were announced by a system of changes. Three times three strokes signified that the departed one was a man; three times two, a woman; twice three, a boy; twice two, a girl. The regular continuity of the tolling suggested that it was the resumption rather than the beginning of a knell—the opening portion of which Stephen had not been near enough to hear.

The momentary anxiety he had felt with regard to his parents passed away. He had left them in perfect health, and had any serious illness seized either, a communication would have reached him ere this. At the same time, since his way homeward lay under the churchyard yews, he resolved to look into the belfry in passing by, and speak a word to Martin Cannister, who would be there.

Stephen reached the brow of the hill, and felt inclined to renounce his idea. His mood was such that talking to any person to whom he could not unburden himself would be wearisome. However, before he could put any inclination into effect, the young man saw from amid the trees a bright light shining, the rays from which radiated like needles through the sad plumy foliage of the yews. Its direction was from the centre of the churchyard.

Stephen mechanically went forward. Never could there be a greater contrast between two places of like purpose than between this graveyard and that of the farther village. Here the grass was carefully tended, and formed virtually a part of the manor-house lawn; flowers and shrubs being planted indiscriminately over both, whilst the few graves visible were mathematically exact in shape and smoothness, appearing in the daytime like chins newly shaven. There was no wall, the division between God's Acre and Lord Luxellian's being marked only by a few square stones set at equidistant points. Among those persons who have romantic sentiments on the subject of their last dwelling-place, probably the greater number would have chosen such a spot as this in preference to any other: a few would have fancied a constraint in its trim neatness, and would have preferred the wild hill-top of the neighbouring site, with Nature in her most negligent attire.

The light in the churchyard he next discovered to have its source in a point very near the ground, and Stephen imagined it might come from a lantern in the interior of a partly-dug grave. But a nearer approach showed him that its position was immediately under the wall of the aisle, and within the mouth of an archway. He could now hear voices, and the truth of the whole matter began to dawn upon him. Walking on towards the opening, Smith discerned on his left hand a heap of earth, and before him a flight of stone steps which the removed earth had uncovered, leading down under the edifice. It was the entrance to a large family vault, extending under the north aisle.

Stephen had never before seen it open, and descending one or two steps stooped to look under the arch. The vault appeared to be crowded with coffins, with the exception of an open central space, which had been necessarily kept free for ingress and access to the sides, round three of which the coffins were stacked in stone bins or niches.

The place was well-lighted with candles stuck in slips of wood that were fastened to the wall. On making the descent of another step the living inhabitants of the vault were recognisable. They were his father the master-mason, an under-mason, Martin Cannister, and two or three young and old labouring-men. Crowbars and workmen's hammers were scattered about. The whole company, sitting round on coffins which had been removed from their places, apparently for some alteration or enlargement of the vault, were eating bread and cheese, and drinking ale from a cup with two handles, passed round from each to each.

'Who is dead?' Stephen inquired, stepping down.

CHAPTER XIII.

'TO THAT LAST NOTHING UNDER EARTH.'

ALL eyes were turned to the entrance as Stephen spoke, and the ancient-mannered conclave scrutinised him inquiringly.

'Why, 'tis our Stephen!' said his father, rising from his seat, and, still retaining the frothy mug in his left hand, swung forward his right for a grasp. 'Your mother is expecting ye—thought you would have come afore dark. But ye'll wait and go home with me? I have all but done for the day, and was going directly.'

'Yes, 'tis Master Stephy, sure enough. Glad to see ye so soon again, Master Smith,' said Martin Cannister, chastening the gladness expressed in his words by a strict neutrality of countenance, in order to harmonise the feeling as much as possible with the solemnity of a position in a family vault.

'The same to you, Martin; and you, William,' said Stephen, nodding around to the rest, who, having their mouths full of bread and cheese, were of necessity compelled to reply merely by looks, which they made friendly by compressing their eyes to lines and wrinkles.

'And who is dead?' Stephen repeated.

'Lady Luxellian, poor gentlewoman, as we all shall,' said the under-mason. 'Ay, and we be going to enlarge the vault to make room for her.'

'When did she die?'

'Early this morning,' his father replied, with an appearance of recurring to a chronic thought. 'Yes, this morning. Martin hev been tolling ever since, almost. There, 'twas expected. She was very limber.'

'Ay, poor gentlewoman, this morning,' resumed the under-mason, a marvellously old man, whose skin seemed so much too large for his body that it would not stay in position. 'She must know by this time whether she's to go up or down, poor gentlewoman.'

'What was her age?'

'Not more than seven or eight-and-twenty by candle-light, poor gentlewoman. But, Lord! by day 'a was forty if 'a were an hour.'

'Ay, nighttime or daytime makes a difference of twenty years to rich feymels,' observed Martin.

'She was one-and-thirty really,' said John Smith. 'I had it from them that know.'

'Not more than that!'

''A looked very bad, poor lady. 'In faith, ye might say she was dead for years afore 'a would own it, poor gentlewoman.'

'As my old father used to say, "dead, but wouldn't drop down."'

'I seed her, poor soul,' said a labourer from behind some removed coffins, 'only but last Valentine's-day of all the world. 'A was arm in crook wi' my lord. I says to myself, "You be ticketed Churchyard, my noble lady, although you don't dream on't."'

'I suppose my lord will write to all the other noble lords anointed in the nation, to let 'em know that she that was is now no more?'

''Tis done and past. I see a bundle go off an hour after the death. Sich wonderful black rims as they letters had—half-an-inch wide, at the very least.'

'Too much,' observed Martin. 'In short, 'tis out of the question that a human being can be so mournful as black edges half-an-inch wide. I'm sure people don't feel more than a very narrow border when they feels most of all.'

'And there are two little girls, are there not?' said Stephen.

'Nice clane little faces!—left motherless now.'

'They used to come to Parson Swancourt's to play with Miss Elfride when I were there,' said William Worm. 'Ah, they did so's!' The latter sentence was introduced to add the necessary melancholy to a remark which, intrinsically, could hardly be made to possess enough for the occasion. 'Yes,' continued Worm, 'they'd run up-stairs, they'd run down; flitting about with her everywhere. Very fond of her, they were. Ah, well!'

'Fonder than ever they were of their mother, so 'tis said here and there,' added a labourer.

'Well, you see, 'tis natural. Lady Luxellian stood aloof from 'em so—was so drowsy-like, that they couldn't love her in the jolly-companion way children want to like folks. Only last winter I seed Miss Elfride talking to my lady and the two children, and Miss Elfride wiped their noses for 'em *so* careful—my lady never once seeing that it wanted doing; and, naturally, children take to people that's their best friend.'

'Be as 'twill, the woman is dead and gone, and we must make a place for her,' said John. 'Come, lads, drink up your ale, and we'll just rid this corner, so as to have all clear for beginning at the wall as soon as 'tis light to-morrow.'

Stephen then asked where Lady Luxellian was to lie.

'Here,' said his father. 'We are going to set back this wall and make a recess; and 'tis enough for us to do before the funeral. When my lord's mother died, she said, "John, the place must be enlarged before another can be put in." But 'a never expected 'twould be wanted so soon. Better move Lord George first, I suppose, Simeon?'

He pointed with his foot to a heavy coffin, covered with what had originally been red velvet, the colour of which could only just be distinguished now.

'Just as ye think best, Master John,'

replied the shrivelled old mason. 'Ah, poor Lord George!' he continued, looking contemplatively at the huge coffin; 'he and I were as bitter enemies once as any could be when one is a lord and t'other only a mortal man. Poor fellow! He'd clap his hand upon my shoulder and cuss me as familiar and neighbourly as if he'd been a common friend. Ay, 'a cussed me up hill and 'a cussed me down; and then 'a would rave out again, and the goold clamps of his fine new teeth would glisten in the sun like fetters of brass, while I, being a small man and poor, was fain to say nothing at all. Such a strappen fine gentleman as he was too! Yes, I rather liked en sometimes. But once now and then, when I looked at his towering height, I'd think in my inside, " What a weight you'll be, my lord, for our arms to lower under the aisle of Endelstow church some day!"'

'And was he?' inquired a young labourer.

'He was. He was five hundredweight if 'a were a pound. What with his lead, and his oak, and his handles, and his one thing and t'other'—here the ancient man slapped his hand upon the cover with a force that caused a rattle among the bones inside—'he half broke my back when I took his feet to lower en down the steps there. "Ah," saith I to John there—didn't I, John?—"that ever one man's glory should be such a weight upon another man!" But there, I liked my Lord George sometimes.'

''Tis a thought to look at,' said another, 'that while they be all here under one roof, a snug and united family of Luxellians, they be really scattered miles away from one another in the form of good sheep and wicked goats, isn't it?'

'True; 'tis a thought to look at.'

'And that one, if he's gone upward, don't know what his wife is doing no more than the man in the moon if she's gone downward. And that some unfortunate one in the hot place is a hollering across to a lucky one up in the clouds, and quite forgetting their bodies be boxed closed together all the time.'

'Ay, 'tis a thought to look at, too, that I can say "Hullo!" close to fiery Lord George, and 'a can't hear me.'

'And that I be eating my onion close to dainty Lady Jane's nose, and she can't smell me.'

'What do 'em put all their heads one way for?' inquired a young man.

'Because 'tis churchyard law, you simple. The law of the living is, that a man shall be upright and downright; and the law of the dead is, that a man shall be cast and west. Every state of society have its laws.'

'We must break the law wi' a few of the poor souls, however. Come, buckle to,' said the master-mason.

And they set to work anew.

The order of interment could be distinctly traced by observing the appearance of the coffins as they lay piled around. On those which had been standing there but a generation or two the trappings still remained. Those of an earlier period showed bare wood, with a few tattered rags dangling therefrom. Earlier still, the wood lay in fragments on the floor of the niche, and the coffin consisted of naked lead alone; whilst in the case of the very oldest, even the lead was bulging and cracking in pieces, revealing to the curious eye a heap of dust within. The shields upon many were quite loose, and removable by the hand, their lustreless surfaces still indistinctly exhibiting the name and title of the deceased.

Overhead the groins and concavities of the arches curved in all directions, dropping low towards the walls, where the height was no more than sufficient to enable a person to stand upright.

The body of George the fourteenth baron, together with two or three others, all of more recent date than the great bulk of coffins piled there, had, for want of room, been placed at the end of the vault on tressels, and not in niches like the others. These it was necessary to remove, to form behind them the chamber in which they were ultimately to be deposited. Stephen, finding the place and proceedings in keeping with the sombre colours of his mind, waited there still.

'Simeon, I suppose you can mind poor Lady Elfride, and how she ran away with the actor?' said John Smith, after a while. 'I think it fell upon the time my father was sexton here. Let us see—where is she?'

'Here somewhere,' returned Simeon, looking round him. 'Why, I've got my arms round the very gentlewoman at this moment.' He lowered the end of the coffin he was holding, wiped his face, and throwing a morsel of rotten wood upon another as an indicator, continued: 'That's her husband, there. They were as fair a couple as you should see anywhere round about; and a good-hearted pair likewise. Ay, I can mind it, though I was but a chiel at the time. She fell in love with this young man of hers, and their banns were asked in some church in London; and the old lord her father actually heard 'em asked the three times, and didn't notice her name, being gabbled on wi' a host of others. When she had married she told her father, and 'a fleed into a monstrous rage, and said she shouldn' hae a farthing. Lady Elfride said she didn't think of wishing it; if he'd forgie her 'twas all she asked, and as for a living, she was content to play plays with her husband. This frightened the old lord, and 'a gie'd 'em a house to live in, and a great garden, and a little field or two, and a carriage, and a good-few guineas. Well, the poor thing died at her first gossiping, and her husband — who was as tender-hearted a man as ever eat meat, and would have died for her—went wild in his mind, and broke his heart (so 'twas said). Anyhow, they were buried the same day—father and mother—but the baby lived. Ay, my lord's family made much of that man then, and put him here with his wife, and there in the corner the man is now. The Sunday after there was a funeral sermon: the text was, "Or ever the silver cord be loosed, or the golden bowl be broken;" and when 'twas preaching the men drew their hands across their eyes several times, and every woman cried out loud.'

'And what became of the baby?' said Stephen, who had frequently heard portions of the story.

'She was brought up by her grandmother, and a pretty maid she were. And she must needs run away with the curate —Parson Swancourt that is now. Then her grandmother died, and the title and everything went away to another branch of the family altogether. Parson Swancourt wasted a good deal of his wife's money, and she left him Miss Elfride. That trick of running away seems to be handed down in families, like craziness or gout. And they two women be alike as peas.'

'Which two?'

'Lady Elfride and young Miss that's alive now. The same hair and eyes: but Miss Elfride's mother was darker a good deal.'

'Life's a strangle bubble, ye see,' said William Worm musingly. 'For if the Lord's anointment had descended upon women instead of men, Miss Elfride would be Lord Luxellian — Lady, I mane. But as it is, the blood is run out, and she's nothing to the Luxellian family by law, whatever she may be by gospel.'

'I used to fancy,' said Simeon, 'when I seed Miss Elfride hugging the little ladyships, that there was a likeness; but I suppose 'twas only my dream, for years must have altered the old family shape.'

'And now we'll move these two, and home-along,' interposed John Smith, reviving, as became a master, the spirit of labour, which had showed unmistakable signs of being nearly vanquished by the spirit of chat. 'The flagon of ale we don't want we'll let bide here till to-morrow; none of the poor souls will touch it 'a b'lieve.'

So the evening's work was concluded, and the party withdrew from the abode of the quiet dead, closing the old iron door, and shooting the lock loudly into the huge copper staple—an incongruous act of imprisonment towards those who had no dreams of escape.

CHAPTER XIV.

'HOW SHOULD I GREET THEE?'

Love frequently dies of time alone—much more frequently of displacement.

With Elfride Swancourt, a powerful reason why the displacement was successful was that the new-comer was a greater man than the first. By the side of the instructive and piquant snubbings she received from Knight, Stephen's general agreeableness seemed watery; by the side of Knight's spare love-making, Stephen's continual outflow seemed lackadaisical. She had begun to sigh for somebody farther on in manliness. Stephen was hardly enough of a man.

Perhaps there was a proneness to inconstancy in her nature—a nature, to those who contemplate it from a standpoint beyond the influence of that inconstancy, the most exquisite of all in its plasticity and ready sympathies. Partly, too, Stephen's failure to make his hold on her heart a permanent one was his too-timid habit of dispraising himself beside her—a peculiarity which, exercised towards sensible men, stirs a kindly chord of attachment that a marked assertiveness would leave untouched, but inevitably leading the most sensible woman in the world to undervalue him who practises it. Directly domineering ceases in the man, snubbing begins in the woman; the trite but no less unfortunate fact being that the gentler creature rarely has the capacity to appreciate fair treatment from her natural complement. The abiding perception of the position of Stephen's parents had, of course, a little to do with Elfride's renunciation. To such girls poverty may not be, as to the more fibrous masses of humanity, a sin in itself; but it is a sin, because graceful and dainty manners seldom exist in such an atmosphere. Few women of old family can be thoroughly taught that a fine soul may wear a smock-frock, and an admittedly common man in one is but a worm in their eyes. John Smith's rough hands and clothes, his wife's dialect, the necessary narrowness of their ways, being constantly under Elfride's notice, were not without their deflecting influence.

On reaching home after the perilous adventure by the sea-shore, Knight had felt unwell, and retired almost immediately. The young lady who had so materially assisted him had done the same, but she reappeared, properly clothed, about five o'clock. She wandered restlessly about the house, but not on account of their joint narrow escape from death. The storm which had torn the tree had merely bowed the reed, and with the deliverance of Knight all deep thought of the accident had left her. The mutual avowal which it had been the means of precipitating occupied a far longer length of her meditations.

Elfride's disquiet now was on account of that miserable promise to meet Stephen, which returned like a spectre again and again. The perception of his littleness beside Knight grew upon her alarmingly. She now thought how sound had been her father's advice to her to give him up, and was as passionately desirous of following it as she had hitherto been averse. Perhaps there is nothing more hardening to the tone of young minds than thus discovering how their dearest and strongest wishes become gradually attuned by Time the Cynic to the very note of some selfish policy which in earlier days they despised.

The hour of appointment came, and with it a crisis; and with the crisis a collapse.

'God forgive me—I can't meet Stephen!' she exclaimed to herself. 'I don't love him less, but I love Mr. Knight more!'

Yes: she would save herself from a

man not fit for her—in spite of vows. She would obey her father, and have no more to do with Stephen Smith. Thus the fickle resolve showed signs of assuming the complexion of a virtue.

The following days were passed without any definite avowal from Knight's lips. Such solitary walks and scenes as that witnessed by Smith in the summer-house were frequent, but he courted her so intangibly, that to any but such a delicate perception as Elfride's it would have appeared no courtship at all. The time now really began to be sweet with her. She dismissed the sense of sin in her past actions, and was automatic in the intoxication of the moment. The fact that Knight made no actual declaration was no drawback. Knowing since the betrayal of his sentiments that love for her really existed, she preferred it for the present in its form of essence, and was willing to avoid for a while the grosser medium of words. Their feelings having been forced to a rather premature demonstration, a reaction was indulged in by both.

But no sooner had she got rid of her troubled conscience on the matter of faithlessness than a new anxiety confronted her. It was lest Knight should accidentally meet Stephen in the parish, and that herself should be the subject of discourse.

Elfride, learning Knight more thoroughly, perceived that, far from having a notion of Stephen's precedence, he had no idea that she had ever been wooed before by anybody. On ordinary occasions she had a tongue so frank as to show her whole mind, and a mind so straightforward as to reveal her heart to its innermost shrine. But the time for a change had come. She never alluded to even a knowledge of Knight's friend. When women are secret they are secret indeed; and more often than not they only begin to be secret with the advent of a second lover.

The elopement was now a spectre worse than the first, and, like the Spirit in Glenfinlas, it waxed taller with every attempt to lay it. Her natural honesty invited her to confide in Knight and trust to his generosity for forgiveness: she knew also that as mere policy it would be better to tell him early if he was to be told at all. The longer her concealment the more difficult would be the revelation. But she put it off. The intense fear which accompanies intense love in young women was too strong to allow the exercise of a moral quality antagonistic to itself:

'Where love is great, the littlest doubts are fear;
Where little fears grow great, great love grows there.'

The match was looked upon as made by her father and mother. The vicar remembered her promise to reveal the meaning of the telegram she had received, and two days after the scene in the summer-house, asked her pointedly. She was frank with him now.

'I had been corresponding with Stephen Smith ever since he left England, till lately,' she calmly said.

'What!' cried the vicar, aghast; 'under the eyes of Mr. Knight, too?'

'No; when I found I cared most for Mr. Knight, I obeyed you.'

'You were very kind, I'm sure. When did you begin to like Mr. Knight?'

'I don't see that that is a pertinent question, papa; the telegram was from the shipping-agent, and was not sent at my request. It announced the arrival of the vessel bringing him home.'

'Home! What, is he here?'

'Yes; in the village, I believe.'

'Has he tried to see you?'

'Only by fair means. But don't, papa, question me so! it is torture.'

'I will only say one word more,' he replied. 'Have you met him?'

'I have not. I can assure you that at the present moment there is no more of an understanding between me and the young man you so much disliked than between him and you. You told me to forget him; and I have forgotten him.'

'O, well; though you did not obey me in the letter, you are a good girl, Elfride, in obeying me at last.'

'Don't call me "good," papa,' she said bitterly; 'you don't know — and the less said about some things the better. Remember, Mr. Knight knows nothing about the other. O, how wrong it all is! I don't know what I am coming to.'

'As matters stand, I should be inclined to tell him; or, at any rate, I should not alarm myself about his knowing. He found out the other day that this was the parish young Smith's father lives in — what puts you in such a flurry?'

'I can't say; but promise — pray don't let him know; it would be my ruin!'

'Pooh, child. Knight is a good fellow and a clever man; but at the same time it does not escape my perceptions that he is no great catch for you. Men of his turn of mind are nothing so wonderful in the way of husbands. If you had chosen to wait, you might have mated with a much wealthier man. But remember, I have not a word to say against your having him, if you like him. Charlotte is delighted, as you know.'

'Well, papa,' she said, smiling hopefully through a sigh, 'it is nice to feel that in giving way to—to caring for him, I have pleased my family. But I am not good; O no, I am very far from that.'

'None of us are good, I am sorry to say,' said her father blandly; 'but girls have a chartered right to change their minds, you know. It has been recognised by poets from time immemorial. Catullus says, "Mulier cupido quod dicit amanti, in vento—" What a memory mine is! However, the passage is, that a woman's words to a lover are as a matter of course written only on wind and water. Now don't be troubled about that, Elfride.'

'Ah, you don't know.'

They had been standing on the lawn, and Knight was now seen lingering some way down a winding walk. When Elfride met him, it was with a much greater lightness of heart; things were more straightforward now. The responsibility of her fickleness seemed partly shifted from her own shoulders to her father's. Still, there were shadows.

'Ah, could he have known how far I went with Stephen, and yet have said the same, how much happier I should be!' That was her prevailing thought.

In the afternoon the lovers went out together on horseback for an hour or two; and though not wishing to be observed, by reason of the late death of Lady Luxellian, whose funeral had taken place very privately on the previous day, they yet found it necessary to pass East Endelstow church.

The steps to the vault, as has been stated, were on the outside of the building, immediately under the aisle wall. Being on horseback, both Knight and Elfride could overlook the shrubs which screened the churchyard.

'Look, the vault seems still to be open,' said Knight.

'Yes, it is open,' she answered.

'Who is that man close by it? The mason, I suppose?'

'Yes.'

'I wonder if it is John Smith, Stephen's father.'

'I believe it is,' said Elfride, with apprehension.

'Ah, and can it be? I should like to inquire how his son, my truant protégé, is going on. And from your father's description of the vault, the interior must be interesting; suppose we go in.'

'Had we better, do you think? May not Lord Luxellian be there?'

'It is not at all likely.'

Elfride then assented, since she could do nothing else. Her heart, which at first had quailed in consternation, recovered itself when she considered the character of John Smith: a quiet unassuming man, he would be sure to act towards her as before those love-passages with his son, which might have given a more pretentious mechanic airs. So without much alarm, she took Knight's arm after dismounting, and went with him between and over the graves. The master-mason recognised her as she approached, and, as usual, lifted his hat respectfully.

'I know you to be Mr. Smith, my former friend Stephen's father,' said Knight, directly he had scanned the embrowned and ruddy features of John.

'Yes, sir, I b'lieve I be.'

'How is your son now? I have only once heard from him since he went to India. I daresay you have heard him speak of me — Mr. Knight, who became acquainted with him some years ago in Casterbridge.'

'Ay, that I have. Stephen is very well, thank you, sir, and he's in England; in fact, he's at home. In short, sir, he's down in the vault there, a-looking at the departed coffins.'

Elfride's heart fluttered like a butterfly.

Knight looked amazed. 'Well, that is extraordinary,' he murmured. 'Did he know I was in the parish?'

'I really can't say, sir,' said John, wishing himself out of the entanglement he rather suspected than thoroughly understood.

'Would it be considered an intrusion by the family if we went into the vault?'

'O, bless ye, no, sir; scores of folk have been stepping down. 'Tis left open a-purpose.'

'We will go down, Elfride.'

'I am afraid the air is close,' she said appealingly.

'O no, ma'am,' said John. 'We white-limed the walls and arches the day 'twas opened, as we always do, and again on the morning of the funeral; the place is as sweet as a granary.'

'Then I should like you to accompany me, Elfie; having originally sprung from the family too.'

'I don't like going where Death is so emphatically present. I'll stay by the horses whilst you go in; they may get loose.'

'What nonsense! I had no idea your sentiments were so flimsily formed as to be perturbed by a few remnants of mortality; but stay out, if you are so afraid, by all means.'

'O no, I am not afraid; don't say that.'

She held miserably to his arm, thinking that, perhaps, the revelation might as well come at once as ten minutes later, for Stephen would be sure to accompany his friend to his horse.

At first, the gloom of the vault, which was lighted only by a couple of tapers, was too great to admit of their seeing anything distinctly; but with a farther advance, Knight discerned, in front of the black masses lining the walls, a young man standing, and writing in a pocket-book.

Knight said one word: 'Stephen!'

Stephen Smith, not being in such absolute ignorance of Knight's whereabouts as Knight had been of Smith's, instantly recognised his friend, and knew by rote the outlines of the fair woman standing behind him.

Stephen came forward and shook him by the hand, without speaking.

'Why have you not written, my boy?' said Knight, without in any way signifying Elfride's presence to Stephen. To the essayist, Smith was still the country lad whom he had patronised and tended; one to whom the formal presentation of a lady betrothed to himself would have seemed incongruous and absurd.

'Why haven't you written to me?' said Stephen.

'Ah, yes. Why haven't I? why haven't we? That's always the query which we cannot clearly answer without an unsatisfactory sense of our inadequacies. However, I have not forgotten you, Smith. And now we have met; and we must meet again, and have a longer chat than this can conveniently be. I must know all you have been doing; that you have thriven, I know, and you must teach me the way.'

Elfride stood in the background. Stephen had read the position at a glance, and immediately guessed that she had never mentioned his name to Knight. His tact in avoiding catastrophes was the chief quality which made him intellectually respectable, in which quality he far transcended Knight; and he decided that a tranquil issue out of the encounter, without any harrowing of the feelings of either Knight or Elfride, was to be attempted if possible. His old sense of indebtedness to Knight had never wholly forsaken him; his love for Elfride was generous now.

As far as he dared look at her movements, he saw that her bearing towards him would be dictated by his own towards her; and if he acted as a stranger, she would do likewise as a means of deliverance. Circumstances favouring this course, it was desirable also to be rather reserved towards Knight, to shorten the meeting as much as possible.

'I am afraid that my time is almost too short to allow even of such a pleasure,' he said. 'I leave here to-morrow. And until I return to India, which will be in a fortnight, I shall have hardly a moment to spare.'

Knight's disappointed and dissatisfied

looks at this reply sent a pang through Stephen as great as any he had felt at the sight of Elfride. The words about shortness of time were literally true, but their tone was far from being so. He would have been gratified to talk with Knight as in past times, and saw as a dead loss to himself that, to save the woman who cared nothing for him, he was deliberately throwing away his friend.

'O, I am sorry to hear that,' said Knight, in a changed tone. 'But of course, if you have weighty concerns to attend to, they must not be neglected. And if this is to be our first and last meeting, let me say that I wish you success with all my heart!' Knight's warmth revived towards the end; the solemn impressions he was beginning to receive from the scene around them abstracting from his heart as a puerility any momentary vexation at words. 'It is a strange place for us to meet in,' he continued, looking round the vault.

Stephen briefly assented, and there was a silence. The blackened coffins were now revealed more clearly than at first, the whitened walls and arches throwing them forward in strong relief. It was a scene which was remembered by all three as an indelible mark in their history. Knight, with an abstracted face, was standing between his companions, though a little in advance of them, Elfride being on his right hand, and Stephen Smith on his left. The white daylight on his right side gleamed faintly in, and was toned to a blueness by contrast with the yellow rays from the candle against the wall. Elfride, timidly shrinking back, and nearest the entrance, received most of the light therefrom, whilst Stephen was entirely in candle-light, and to him the spot of outer sky visible above the steps was as a steely blue patch, and nothing more.

'I have been here two or three times since it was opened,' said Stephen. 'My father was engaged in the work, you know.'

'Yes. What are you doing?' Knight inquired, looking at the note-book and pencil Stephen held in his hand.

'I have been sketching a few details in the church, and since then I have been copying the names from some of the coffins here. Before I left England, I used to do a good deal of this sort of thing.'

'Yes; of course. Ah, that's poor Lady Luxellian, I suppose.' Knight pointed to a coffin of light satin-wood, which stood on the stone sleepers in the new niche. 'And the remainder of the family are on this side. Who are those two, so snug and close together?'

Stephen's voice altered slightly as he replied: 'That's Lady Elfride Kingsmore —born Luxellian, and that is Arthur, her husband. I have heard my father say that they—he—ran away with her, and married her against the wish of her parents.'

'Then I imagine this to be where you got your Christian name, Miss Swancourt?' said Knight, turning to her. 'I think you told me it was three or four generations ago that your family branched off from the Luxellians?'

'She was my grandmother,' said Elfride, vainly endeavouring to moisten her dry lips before she spoke. Elfride had then the conscience-stricken look of Guido's Magdalen, rendered upon a more childlike form. She kept her face partially away from Knight and Stephen, and set her eyes upon the sky visible outside, as if her salvation depended upon quickly reaching it. Her left hand rested lightly within Knight's arm, half withdrawn, from a sense of shame at claiming him before her old lover, yet unwilling to renounce him; so that her glove merely touched his sleeve. 'Can one be pardoned, and retain the offence?' said Elfride's heart then.

Conversation seemed to have no self-sustaining power, and went on in the shape of disjointed remarks. 'One's mind gets thronged with thoughts whilst standing so solemnly here,' Knight said, in a measured quiet voice. 'How much has been said on death from time to time! how much we ourselves can think upon it! We may fancy each of these who lie here saying:

> "For Thou, to make my fall more great,
> Didst lift me up on high."

What comes next, Elfride? It is the Hundred-and-second Psalm I am thinking of.'

'Yes, I know it,' she murmured, and went on in a still lower voice, seemingly afraid for any words from the emotional side of her nature to reach Stephen:

> '"My days, just hastening to their end,
> Are like an evening shade;
> My beauty doth, like wither'd grass,
> With waning lustre fade."'

'Well,' said Knight musingly, 'let us

leave them. Such occasions as these seem to compel us to roam outside ourselves, far away from the fragile frame we live in, and to expand till our perception grows so vast that our physical reality bears no sort of proportion to it. We look back upon the weak and minute stem on which this luxuriant growth depends, and ask, Can it be possible that such a capacity has a foundation so small? Must I again return to my daily walk in that narrow cell, a human body, where worldly thoughts can torture me? Do we not?'

'Yes,' said Stephen and Elfride.

'One has a sense of wrong, too, that such an appreciative breadth as a sentient being possesses should be committed to the frail casket of a body. What weakens one's intentions regarding the future like the thought of this? .... However, let us tune ourselves to a more cheerful chord, for there's a great deal to be done yet by us all.'

As Knight meditatively addressed his juniors thus, unconscious of the deception practised, for different reasons, by the severed hearts at his side, and of the scenes that had in earlier days united them, each one felt that he and she did not gain by contrast with their musing mentor. Physically not so handsome as either the youthful architect or the vicar's daughter, the thoroughness and integrity of Knight illuminated his features with a dignity not even incipient in the other two. It is difficult to frame rules which shall apply to both sexes, and Elfride, an undeveloped girl, can hardly be laden with the moral responsibilities which attach to a man under like circumstances. The charm of woman, too, lies partly in her subtleness in matters of love. But if honesty is a virtue in itself, Elfride, having none of it now, seemed, being for being, scarcely good enough for Knight. Stephen, though deceptive for no unworthy purpose, was deceptive after all; and whatever good results grace such strategy if it succeed, it seldom draws admiration, especially when it fails.

On an ordinary occasion, had Knight been even quite alone with Stephen, he would hardly have alluded to his possible relationship to Elfride. But moved by attendant circumstances, Knight was impelled to be confiding.

'Stephen,' he said, 'this lady is Miss Swancourt. I am staying at her father's house, as you probably know.' He stepped a few paces nearer to Smith, and said in a lower tone: 'I may as well tell you that we are engaged to be married.'

Low as the words had been spoken, Elfride had heard them, and awaited Stephen's reply in breathless silence, if that could be called silence where Elfride's dress, at each throb of her heart, shook and indicated it like a pulse-glass, rustling also against the wall in reply to the same throbbing. The ray of daylight which reached her face lent it a blue pallor in comparison with those of the other two.

'I congratulate you,' Stephen whispered; and said aloud, 'I know Miss Swancourt— a little. You must remember that my father is a parishioner of Mr. Swancourt's.'

'I thought you might possibly not have lived at home since they have been here,' said Knight.

'I have never lived at home, certainly, since that time.'

'I have seen Mr. Smith,' faltered Elfride.

'Well, there is no excuse for me. As strangers to each other I ought, I suppose, to have presented you: as acquaintances, I should not have stood so persistently between you. But the fact is, Smith, you seem a boy to me, even now.'

Stephen appeared to have a more than previous consciousness of the intense cruelty of his fate at the present moment. He could not repress the words, uttered with a dim bitterness:

'You should have said that I seemed still the rural mechanic's son I am, and hence an unfit subject for the ceremony of introductions.'

'O, no, no! I won't have that.' Knight endeavoured to give his reply a laughing tone in Elfride's ears, and an earnestness in Stephen's: in both which efforts he signally failed, and produced a forced speech pleasant to neither. 'Well, let us go into the open air again; Miss Swancourt, you are particularly silent. You mustn't mind Smith. I have known him for years, as I have told you.'

'Yes, you have,' she said.

'To think she has never mentioned her knowledge of me!' Smith murmured, and thought with some remorse how much her conduct resembled his own on his first arrival at her house as a stranger to the place.

They ascended to the daylight, Knight taking no further notice of Elfride's manner, which, as usual, he attributed to the natural shyness of a young female at being discovered walking with him on terms which left not much doubt of their meaning. Elfride stepped a little in advance, and passed through the churchyard.

'You are changed very considerably, Smith,' said Knight, 'and I suppose it is no more than was to be expected. However, don't imagine that I shall feel any the less interest in you and your fortunes whenever you care to confide them to me. I have not forgotten the attachment you spoke of as your reason for going away to India. A London young lady, was it not? I hope all is prosperous?'

'No: the match is broken off.'

It being always difficult to know whether to express sorrow or gladness under such circumstances—all depending upon the character of the match—Knight took shelter in the safe words: 'I trust it was for the best.'

'I hope it was. But I beg that you

will not press me farther: no, you have not pressed me—I don't mean that—but I would rather not speak upon the subject.'

Stephen's words were hurried.

Knight said no more, and they followed in the footsteps of Elfride, who still kept some paces in advance, and had not heard Knight's unconscious allusion to her. Stephen bade him adieu at the churchyard-gate without going outside, and watched whilst he and his sweetheart mounted their horses.

'Good heavens, Elfride,' Knight exclaimed, 'how pale you are! I suppose I ought not to have taken you into that vault. What is the matter?'

'Nothing,' said Elfride faintly. 'I shall be myself in a moment. All was so strange and unexpected down there, that it made me faint.'

'I thought you said very little. Shall I get some water?'

'No, no.'

'Do you think it is safe for you to mount?'

'Quite—indeed it is,' she said, with a look of appeal.

'Now then—up she goes!' whispered Knight, and lifted her tenderly into the saddle.

Her old lover still looked on at the performance as he leant over the gate a dozen yards off. Once in the saddle, and having a firm grip of the reins, she turned her head as if by a resistless fascination, and for the first time since that memorable parting on the moor outside St. Kirrs, after the passionate attempt at marriage with him, Elfride looked in the face of the young man she first had loved. He was the youth who had called her his inseparable wife many a time, and whom she had even addressed as her husband. Their eyes met. Measurement of life should be proportioned rather to the intensity of the experience therein contained than to its actual length.

Their glance, but a moment chronologically, was a season in their history. To Elfride the intense agony of reproach in Stephen's eye was a nail piercing her heart with a deadliness no words can describe. With a spasmodic effort she withdrew her eyes, urged on the horse, and in the chaos of perturbed memories was oblivious of any presence beside her. The deed of deception was complete.

Gaining a knoll on which the park transformed itself into wood and copse, Knight came still closer to her side, and said, 'Are you better now, dearest?'

'O, yes.' She pressed a hand to her eyes, as if to blot out the image of Stephen. A vivid scarlet spot now shone with preternatural brightness in the centre of each cheek, leaving the remainder of her face lily-white as before.

'Elfride,' said Knight, rather in his old tone of mentor, 'you know I don't for a moment chide you, but is there not a great deal of unwomanly weakness in your allowing yourself to be so overwhelmed by the sight of what, after all, is no novelty? Every woman worthy of the name should, I think, be able to look upon death with something like composure. Surely you think so too?'

'Yes; I own it.'

His obtuseness to the cause of her indisposition, by evidencing his entire freedom from the suspicion of anything behind the scenes, showed how incapable Knight was of deception himself, rather than any inherent dulness in him regarding human nature. This, clearly perceived by Elfride, added poignancy to her self-reproach, and she idolised him the more because of their difference. Even the recent sight of Stephen's face and the sound of his voice, which for a moment had stirred a chord or two of ancient kindness, were unable to keep down the adoration reëxistent now that he was again out of view.

She had replied to Knight's question hastily, and immediately went on to speak of indifferent subjects. After they had reached home, she was apart from him till dinner-time. When dinner was over, and they were watching the dusk in the drawing-room, Knight stepped out upon the terrace. Elfride went after him very decisively, on the spur of a virtuous intention.

'Mr. Knight, I want to tell you something,' she said, with quiet firmness.

'And what is it about?' gaily returned her lover. 'Happiness, I hope. Do not let anything keep you so sad as you seem to have been to-day.'

'I cannot mention the matter until I tell you the whole substance of it,' she said. 'And that I will do to-morrow. I have been reminded of it to-day. It is about something I once did, and don't think I ought to have.'

This, it must be said, was rather a mild way of referring to a frantic passion and flight, which, much or little in itself, only accident had saved from being a scandal in the public eye.

Knight thought the matter some trifle, and said pleasantly:

'Then I am not to hear the dreadful confession now?'

'No, not now. I did not mean to-night,' Elfride responded, with a slight decline in the firmness of her voice. 'It is not light, as you think it—it troubles me a great deal.' Fearing now the effect of her own earnestness, she added forcedly, 'Though, perhaps, you may think it light after all.'

'But you have not said when it is to be?'

'To-morrow morning. Name a time, will you, and bind me to it? I want you to name an hour, because I am weak, and may otherwise try to get out of it.' She added a little artificial laugh, which showed how timorous her resolution was still.

'Well, say after breakfast — at eleven o'clock.'

'Yes, eleven o'clock. I promise you. Bind me strictly to my word.'

END OF VOL. II.